CREATIVITY
AND
SUCCESSFUL
INNOVATION

Roy,

Best wishes.

Larry R. [signature]

2/10/2012

Larry R. Marshall, Ph.D.

This book is based solely on the
experiences of Larry R. Marshall.
It is intended to be the first in a series of books
about creativity and innovation.

First Edition: December, 2010

Library of Congress Control Number: 2010908356

ISBN-10 Number 1453618864
ISBN-13 Number 9781453618868

Cover design and typesetting by Ashley Snead
Cover illustration: liquidlibrary 033C0103LL.eps

Printed by CreateSpace

Dedication

To my wife, Jo Ann, for her support all these years in my lifelong quest to learn how to be creative and how to convert creative thoughts and ideas into reality through successful innovation. Also to our twins, Shelly and John, who have pursued careers other than science and engineering and hopefully will find this work applicable in their fields of endeavor as well. But mainly this work is dedicated to our grandchildren, Graham, Nicolas, McKenzie, and Samuel; in the hope that as the twenty-first century unfolds, coincident with their lives and careers, they will revisit this work occasionally and find it applicable and relevant.

IV

Acknowledgements

First, I wish to acknowledge my parents, Ray and Lillian, for giving me the desire to learn and for encouraging me "to get an education." I was fortunate to grow up close to Virginia Tech which enabled me to attend as a day student. I will always be appreciative for those leaders in the 1800s who established low tuition, land grant universities making it possible some 100 years later for me to get that education. Following graduation as an aerospace engineer, the Boeing Company gave me the dream job of working on the Apollo Program in Huntsville, Alabama. The University of Alabama in Huntsville allowed me to attend graduate school while working at Boeing, and also hired me as an engineer when employment in the space industry was no longer possible. Therefore, I wish to acknowledge the Boeing Company and the University of Alabama in Huntsville for the fantastic, once-in-a-lifetime experience to be a part of Apollo and experience the electrifying atmosphere of the space program. I then decided to return to Virginia Tech and exit the aerospace industry for a career in the general sciences of engineering. I continue to be extremely grateful to Dr. Daniel Frederick, Head of the Department of Engineering Science and Mechanics, for granting me a Fellowship which allowed me to pursue any topic of my choosing for my Doctoral Dissertation. The Fellowship made it possible for me to work on Nonlinear Ship Motions under Dr. Dean T. Mook. The driving force behind the research into nonlinear mechanics at that time was Dr. Ali Nayfeh, who also was my advisor. It was during this time that I gained confidence that I could work successfully in the field of research and development, and I therefore acknowledge both Dr. Mook and Dr. Nayfeh for their help and guidance in my graduate research. I then went to work for the DuPont Company which granted me the opportunity to work on important business relevant problems requiring creativity and successful innovation over a 34 year career. At DuPont I worked with many talented scientists, engineers, and managers. I wish to thank Dr. John Farago for mentoring me during my early years and teaching me the value of compromise in order to get a project successfully accomplished. I will always remember working with highly competent engineers like: Dr. Thomas Bednarz, Dr. Thomas Morrow, Dr. Michael Bryner, Kent Horner, Michael Davis, Amanda Miller, William Hommes, Gale Wheeler, and Robert Marin. I thank them for the many years of collaboration and mutual learning. I was also fortunate to have great managerial support from Charles Prather, John Hutchinson, Ralph Franke, Roger Siemionko, and Lewis Manring. I thank Ashley Snead for typesetting this book and for her creative cover design. And finally, I wish to thank Jean Welch, Nathan Cain, Jessica Baake, Robert Marin, Michael Marin, and Johan Brag for reading drafts of this book and providing suggestions for improvement.

Contents

Preface

The focus of this book is SUCCESS – success achieved from transforming creativity into successful innovations. In this book, I discuss the application of techniques that helped me be successful in commercializing many innovations at the DuPont Company during a career lasting over thirty years. I started making notes about my techniques in 2002 and first referred to these techniques as "Larry's Laws" because of the catchiness of this phrase. As I made notes, I realized that I had developed these "Laws" as my career went along, not all at once. Many of them resulted from successfully dealing with the frustrations that are a necessary part of the innovative process. Some of them came from reflecting back on various development projects and taking note of what worked well and what was helpful in bringing the project to a successful conclusion. A couple of the "Laws" resulted from comparing my techniques with those of colleagues that never seemed to be very successful. I also compared my techniques to those of other colleagues that always seemed to be successful. As I contemplated writing a book describing my techniques; I asked the question: "am I qualified to write a book giving advice on innovation and creativity?" To answer this question, I decided to calculate my rate of success over my thirty year career at DuPont. For the calculation, I established these criteria:

1) For a project to be successful it had to be commercialized in one of DuPont's plants,

2) I had to have worked on the project for about two years, which means that I put a serious effort into it,

3) And most of all, the project required innovating technology that had never been done before.

I was somewhat surprised when I calculated a 71% success rate. The usual rule of thumb that seems widely accepted is that R&D projects enjoy a 10% rate of success. Feeling that I was qualified to write a book on creativity and innovation and believing that I could indeed contribute to the knowledge base on these subjects, I first copyrighted the following "Laws" in 2003:

LARRY'S LAWS

OF

SUCCESSFUL INNOVATION

AND

CREATIVITY©

1. The overriding law of successful innovation is maintaining a "wanting to do it attitude."

2. It is more difficult to determine that something cannot be done than it is to determine that it can be done.

3. Learn more from ideas that do not work than you learn from ideas that do work.

4. Do your best work when things look the bleakest.

5. Strive for the simplest approach by asking "what would a man-on-the-street think and do when faced with this difficult situation?"

6. Successful innovation is best accomplished with partial realization of great ideas; therefore, practice compromise, declare victory, and move on.

7. When things get difficult, do not try to force good ideas – just let them happen.

8. Learn to listen – you just never know where a good idea will come from.

9. Always be striving for creative ideas at a higher level – especially when things are going well.

10. Successful out-of-the-box thinking requires – first having been in-the-box.

11. An innovator's greatest fear should be – missing a path to success.

Larry's Laws of Successful Innovation and Creativity©

12. Never think a negative thought and never totally believe what people tell you.

13. Complex innovations require that success be achieved in steps, versus all at once.

14. Measure your success by setting a few intermediate milestones to coincide with a step-by-step approach.

15. Always develop multiple paths to success with as many back-ups as possible.

16. Practice diversity in thinking by always having side projects.

17. Success results from thinking the right kind of thoughts, doing the right things, and making the right decisions.

18. Thinking the right kind of thoughts keeps you in the game, doing the right things and making the right decisions win the game.

Over the last eight years I have continued to draft this book as time allowed. The book develops each "Law" presented above into a chapter describing how to apply that "Law" in the real world of business. During this process, I realized that a Chapter on the necessity of being at risk should be added. Because in the world of business, the innovator has to put his ideas and career at risk in order to turn creative ideas into business successes.

Prior to the chapters on the "Laws" or techniques, I introduce the book with a discussion on what constitutes a business cycle of a successful innovation in Chapter 1. In that chapter I present the concept of an Innovation Development Curve which precedes the typical "S-curve" life cycle of a successful product, service, or process (see the Definitions section of this book for an explanation of an "S-curve"). In Chapter 1, I also present suggested times to use the techniques of this book relative to where the innovator is along the Innovation Development Curve.

After showing a very early draft of this book to my grandson Graham, he suggested that I add a section in each chapter about my "personal experiences."

The first edition of this book has been written without a great deal of reference to existing literature on methods of innovation and creativity. I decided to do it that way so that I could be sure that the ideas presented herein were a result of my personal experiences and not the result of someone else's personal experiences. It is my intent to write a second edition in which the contents of this book will be connected to the general body of knowledge on innovation and creativity.

Therefore, the intent of this book is to present my "Laws of Successful Innovation and Creativity" with the sincere hope that you learn to use them to improve your percentage of successful development projects.

Definitions

Understanding the following definitions will be helpful as you read this book.

Creativity

Creativity means the act of conceiving original things. These things can be ideas, concepts, designs, etc.

Innovation

Innovation means the process of turning creativity into reality. Reality can be products, services, processes, etc.

Quality Function Deployment (QFD)

Quality Function Deployment, or QFD, means establishing the critical commercial requirements (and associated metrics for success) of a product, service, or process that is to be innovated.

Concurrent Engineering (CE)

Concurrent engineering is a process for ensuring that customer requirements are ascertained prior to the start of a project (QFD) and that work is carried on concurrently on the various disciplines involved and on the various steps of the innovation according to an overall development plan. The CE process also establishes a metric of success for each specific or functional requirement. The CE process can be applied to establish design specifications for either product or process innovation.

Rack-up

Rack-up means the methodology of summarizing, or condensing, a very difficult problem or situation into its simplest, most concise form for analysis. It is essential that the analyst does the rack-up in an unbiased way.

S-curve

The "S-curve" is a graphical representation of the life cycle of a successful product, service, or process. First there is a slow-growth time period following commercialization when the product, service, or process is getting established. Then the product, service, or process experiences a time period of rapid growth and acceptance. Finally, the product, service, or process ends its useful life during a time period when growth has stopped and it is replaced by newly innovated technology.

80-20 Rule

The 80-20 rule means that sometimes 80% of ultimate success can be attained with 20% of the effort that it would take to achieve ultimate success. Thus, since speed to market is critical for new innovations to be successful, attaining 80% of theoretical success in 20% of the time is usually a great compromise.

Chapter 1

Business Cycle of a Successful Innovation

Creativity and Successful Innovation are the core activities that create and sustain the world's premier business enterprises.

A successful business cycle is comprised of an innovative phase followed by a commercial phase.

◆ Creativity transformed into successful innovation is the source of businesses' new products, services, and processes.

◆ The business cycles of new products, services, and processes are comprised of an innovation phase followed by a commercial phase.

◆ The innovation phase proceeds along an innovation development curve and the commercial phase follows the well known life cycle "S-curve."

◆ An innovation development curve expresses the probability of success and the degree of risk relative to the amount of time required to achieve successful innovation from a creative idea or concept.

◆ The successful innovator employs techniques that will enhance the probability of success and reduce the degree of risk while striving to shorten the timeline from creative idea to start of commercialization.

◆ The techniques presented in this book are intended to help the innovator reduce the level of risk while shortening the timeline to start of the commercial phase.

Innovation Development Curve

A successful business cycle is made up of an innovation phase followed by a commercial phase. The innovation phase, the subject of this book, starts with the creative idea or concept for a new product, service, or process and ends when it has undergone development into commercial reality and is ready to be sold, provided, or practiced. The commercial phase starts when the newly innovated product, service, or process is first sold, provided, or practiced by customers and typically undergoes what is referred to as an "S-curve" of commercial life experience until it is replaced by a more innovative product, service, or process. The "S-curve" means that at first, sales ramp up gradually, then sales hit their stride during a period of rapid growth, and finally the sales level off during the later part of the commercial phase. A graphical depiction of these two phases is presented in Figure 1.

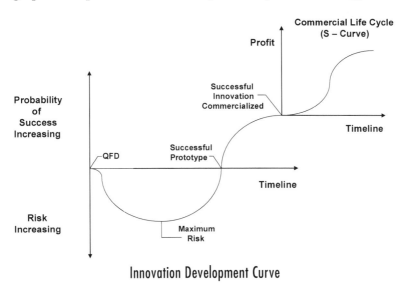

Innovation Development Curve

Figure 1   Phases of a Successful Innovation

The innovative phase is expressed as an innovation development curve with two scales reflecting the degree of risk undertaken versus time and the probability of success versus time. The commercial phase is expressed as an "S-curve" relationship between profit and time.

The level of risk can be reduced from the very beginning by performing what is called the Quality Function Deployment (QFD) process. This is a method for determining the specific requirements of the product, service, or process to be innovated. If a complete QFD cannot be done, then the innovator must make whatever effort possible to ensure that the right things are being worked on from the beginning of the project.

As the innovation process gets into full swing, the level of risk undertaken by the innovator will continue to increase with time as resources are expended, experiments are run, and data are analyzed. In every development, the innovator will face a time when the success of the development is in serious doubt – this is when the risk is at a maximum. If the development is to be successful, positive results will be obtained and the level of risk will start decreasing. The cross-over point of the innovation development curve is when a proof-of-concept sample has been made, or a successful service or process prototype is demonstrated. Once a successful proof-of-concept sample, service, or prototype is demonstrated, the curve reflects that the proper focus should be achieving commercial success and that the development should be assessed in terms of its probability of success.

Enterprise survival ultimately depends on the speed at which new innovations can be commercialized. The enterprise that wins the game is the one with the shortest timelines for successful innovations. This book presents techniques that are aimed at helping the innovator reduce the level of risk and shorten the timeline to commercialization. Figure 2 presents an Innovation Development Curve with a shortened timeline and reduced level of risk.

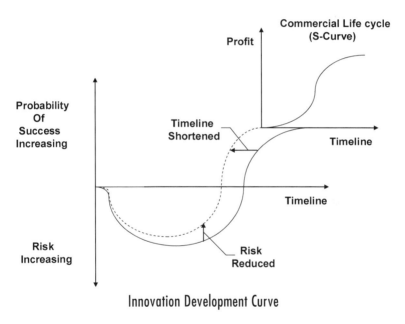

Figure 2   Shortening the Timeline to Successful Innovation using the Techniques of this Book

There are nineteen techniques presented in this book for helping the innovator be successful and these are described in Chapters 3 -21. Chapter 2 discusses the necessity of being at risk and is not considered a technique per se. Chapters 3-21 are arranged in the order that they should be consulted as the innovator proceeds along the Innovation Development Curve. The approximate times for consultation of the chapters are shown in Figure 3. Of course the creative innovator may consult any chapter at any time for additional insight into successful innovation. Also shown in Figure 3 is a general idea of which chapters pertain to the creative process and which chapters pertain to the innovation process.

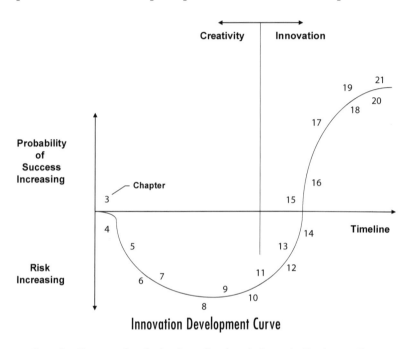

Figure 3   Chapters to Consult when Proceeding along the Innovation Development Curve

Personal Experience

During my career at the DuPont Company, I had the opportunity to embark along the Innovation Development Curve about 20 times. I was fortunate to have achieved successful innovation many times by commercializing over 70% of those projects. I continue to thank DuPont and all the talented people that worked at DuPont for supporting me and helping me to be successful. While I worked at DuPont, I always felt that I had one of the best jobs in the world in terms of having challenging projects and managerial support to pursue my work as I learned to be creative and turn that creativity into business success. As I now look back at my experiences, I realize that few people get the opportunities that I had at DuPont. It was a combination of corporate support, business need, and my personal comfort with putting my career and ideas at risk in order to achieve successful innovation (see Chapter 2).

In terms of achieving successful innovation, the importance of quickly making a proof of concept sample or a successful prototype cannot be overstated. This is the most important thing to be accomplished along the Innovation Development Curve. It is so important to demonstrate this milestone that even if it takes making the sample or prototype via a surrogate technology, then that is allowable. Allowable as long as the innovator knows that the primary technology will make a similar sample or prototype. The reason I stress this approach is that I was once working on a difficult technology innovation and I focused primarily on the technology development aspects, versus making a product proof of concept sample. I did not realize that the funding organization needed the proof of concept sample to properly value the potential of the innovation. As a result, the project was stopped. Looking back on that experience, I realize now that I could have easily made a proof of concept sample another way and most likely the project would have been carried to a successful conclusion. Although the funding organization did not get a successful innovation, the basic technology of the innovation is "on the shelf." As discussed in Chapter 6, past work that has been "tabled" is an especially rich source of information in large organizations with great potential value. Thus making a successful prototype or proof of sample can be of value when innovated or "tabled" to a later time.

Chapter 2

The Necessity of Being at Risk

You have to put at risk both your creative ideas
and your career in order to have one of
life's most exhilarating experiences –
successful innovation, accomplished
after persevering and overcoming
all the obstacles and frustration
along the way.

Being at Risk is a Necessary Part of Achieving Successful Innovations from Creative Ideas.

♦ Innovators are creators and make the world a better place.

♦ Successful innovators will take the risks necessary to pursue their creative ideas without concern of criticism or fear of perceived failure.

♦ Successful innovators must also be capable of persevering and overcoming the frustration of a risky development process, often over a long period of time.

♦ Thus, managing and embracing risk is essential to the innovation process.

♦ Therefore, the constant state of being at risk is a necessary part of successful innovation.

The Necessity of Being at Risk

As you read this book you will find out that I believe only positive thinking people can be successful innovators. This is because of the tremendous difficulty in converting creative concepts and ideas into innovations that really work. Overcoming and working through the difficulties requires great determination, which in turn requires the constant belief that anything can be accomplished. I have found that very few people share this view of things, but rather view the innovative process as extremely risky in terms of being subjected to personal criticism when things are perceived as not going well. Large corporations have exacerbated this situation by making managers, engineers, and scientific personnel perceive the downside risk for working on innovations as being greater than the upside reward for successful innovations. It is now, as I look back on my career, that I realize that being at risk is a necessary part of achieving successful innovations from creative concepts and ideas. In my opinion, innovators in the arts, such as writers and painters, seem to have accepted "the necessity of being at risk" more readily than the scientific community – certainly more so than the engineering community.

I also believe that there is no such thing as failure, only setbacks that are part of the process of creativity and innovation. Learning from these setbacks and feeding that new knowledge back into the development of better ideas requires a great ability to deal with frustration – often over long periods of time – which can mean too much risk for most people. Something that has always helped me to get through these periods of frustration is to remind myself that I had to do my best work when things looked the bleakest (Chapter 8).

Another important thing I have learned is that great ideas cannot be forced, they just have to happen. Of course when I put it that way, it does not mean that little effort is put into the quest for better ideas; in fact, just the opposite must be done as you search for alternate approaches. You have to learn to listen, develop multiple back up plans, follow up on every lead, and practice truly getting out of the box. All this kind of work takes time and it can appear to outsiders that not much is happening on your project because results are not forthcoming at regular intervals – thus you risk poor performance evaluations if you work in a major corporation or organization.

I have found that developing multiple paths to success is an important way to reduce risk since relying on only one path is foolhardy. The development of what I call side projects is essential for diversifying your thinking and renewing your attitude. Very often a major project will result from someone's side project – this has happened to me several times. However, while I believe that side projects reduce risk, the development of such projects can be viewed as distracting from your goals and objectives by outsiders and thus you again risk lower performance ratings as a result if you work in a large organization.

Ultimately, successful innovation comes down to thinking the right kind of thoughts and making the right decisions. The perceptions of outsiders are certainly risks, but have no direct impact on reality except in terms of limiting resources to the innovator which can certainly be a factor. Therefore, managing the perception of risk enters into making the right decisions. I have found that this risk is mitigated as long as it is clear that the innovator is working on a project that is clearly aimed at the business success of the funding enterprise.

In summary, risk is an essential part of the innovation process and the successful innovator must learn to manage and embrace it. However, while successful innovation will not occur without risk, an interesting situation happens as success is within sight – the successful innovator must make the right decision by reducing the state of risk and taking only the conservative, prudent risks required to achieve success. This is discussed in Chapter 21.

Personal Experience

I suppose the reason I am comfortable with risk is that I have been at risk my whole life. In fact, I am uncomfortable when I am not at risk. This probably goes back to my life being concurrent with the "space race" between the United States and Russia. Back then, Americans were comfortable with taking the risk of a rocket blowing up during launch because they knew it to be a necessary part of the development process of winning the space race. The country was run by people fresh from winning World War II, a time when our whole country and future were at risk. Therefore, they accepted risk as part of their work. I grew up in that environment; loved the thought of going into outer space, and got my degree in Aerospace Engineering with that intention. My first job as a professional engineer was on the Apollo Program for the Boeing Company. I was mesmerized by the "electric atmosphere" surrounding the Apollo Project – I felt it both in Huntsville, Alabama and in Cape Canaveral, Florida. I remember a trip that I took to Cape Canaveral in 1968. It was my first airplane flight; and I was super excited to see first-hand the Saturn V rocket. There were 3 Saturn Vs being assembled in the Vehicle Assembly Building as far as I remember. For a young aerospace engineer, this was all that I had dreamed of as I grew up. The physical scale and intensity of the Apollo Program, combined with the new science of space exploration and its inherent risks, created the "electric atmosphere" of America's space program. Then, when we won the space race and landed on the moon in July, 1969, the electricity went away. Unfortunately for America, the electricity has not returned.

I experienced similar "electric" situations during my career at DuPont. That is a goal has to be accomplished that is so important that everyone working on it realizes that success is the only acceptable outcome. This happened to me twice. In one case, I was totally responsible for the project's success. In the other, I was a team member. Both were successful for different reasons, and I have drawn on my experiences from these projects to develop the principles put forth in this book. Similar to the space race, these projects had a goal that was clear to all involved – everyone bought into devoting whatever effort it took to be successful. Then when success was achieved, life returned to "normal;" the business enterprise experienced great financial reward, and those that accomplished the success went their own way looking to contribute to another such project. The problem, of course, is there are few such projects because they are born out of either creativity or necessity. Creativity – when an enterprise happens upon an invention that offers the chance to grow organically. Necessity – when an enterprise is faced with survival.

Dealing with great personal risk was a part of my experience in both of these projects at DuPont. The one where I was totally responsible, I did all the technical work and invention, and converted commercial plants to higher capacities. The project where I was a team member, I did some of the technical work and invention and led engineering teams to build new process technologies. The many other projects I worked on at DuPont were a combination of personal and team efforts. Now looking back on my career at DuPont, I realize that being comfortable with putting myself at risk enabled me to become a creative person and sustained me during the very difficult times required to convert creativity into successful innovations.

Chapter 3

Maintaining a "Wanting to Do It" Attitude

The closer you get to the mountaintop, the heavier the load, and the greater the determination required for success.

The overriding law of successful innovation and creativity is maintaining a "wanting to do it" attitude.

♦ In real estate it's location, location, location.
  In innovation it's attitude, attitude, attitude.

♦ Attitude overrides everything: education, talent, resources, …

♦ Successful innovation results from conversion of positive thinking into the perseverance necessary to maintain a "wanting to do it attitude."

♦ Thus, it's attitude, perseverance, and wanting to get it done that lead to successful innovation.

Maintaining a "Wanting to Do It" Attitude

The most important personal trait enabling successful innovation is maintaining a "wanting to do it" attitude. Creativity requires other traits and techniques. But to be successful at converting creativity into innovation, it's your attitude that is most important. In fact, attitude overrides education, talent, and resources. However the innovator that combines education, talent, and resources with a determined attitude will increase his/her chances for successful innovation. Mastering the techniques presented in this book will further increase the innovator's chances.

Most of the world's great innovators possess an unrelenting attitude to make their projects successful. They are not discouraged by setbacks and maintain their "wanting to do it" attitude no matter what problems they encounter. It takes experience to know that maintaining the proper attitude will ultimately lead to success. Once an innovator experiences success, he/she becomes addicted to the process of converting creativity into successful innovation. Life is never the same again, and each successful innovation will build upon the previous one to improve the innovator's success rate. The innovator will look back at how maintaining a "wanting to do it" attitude led to project success and that will only intensify his/her positive attitude the next time around.

Maintaining a "wanting to do it" attitude basically means making a personal commitment to successfully completing one's project as long as ethical principles and the laws of physics are not violated. Once this personal commitment has been made, the hard part starts. And this is where the techniques, or "Laws," presented in this book, come into play. They are intended to help the innovator be successful by offering ways to approach extremely difficult problems, regardless of the field of endeavor. These "Laws" do not adhere to the concepts of: 1) failing early on a project so that the innovator can move on to another project with a perceived higher probability of success or 2) finding a show stopper which means determining that there is some fundamental barrier to successfully accomplishing the project. One must maintain the view that there is no obstacle that cannot be dealt with in a successful way. Determining ways or paths to success requires that thoughts should be thought other than the purely specific fundamentals of the sciences involved. Thinking the "right kinds of thoughts" will keep the innovator in the game and ultimately lead to successful innovation and creativity.

Personal Experience

During the course of my career, I have found that not many people can deal with the seemingly continual frustration of research and development work. Many of the "Laws" discussed in this book deal with techniques I have developed to help overcome one's frustrations and yet maintain the "wanting to do it" attitude. I recall saying to myself many times over the years simple things like, "do your best work when things look the bleakest" or "learn more from things that do not work than from things that do work." I always felt better following these "mental pep talks." Conversely, when an experiment was successful, I would experience the exhilaration for a while and then remind myself that "I should be striving for additional creative ideas at a higher level" or "developing another path to success" because one cannot have enough back-up plans.

My greatest professional success has been scaling up very complex commercial processes so that they ran faster and increased production. This was very difficult work because the experiments were conducted on commercial scale equipment and any upset in production would cause downtime and the loss of millions of dollars. The mental stress was almost unbearable because I knew that my career hinged on the success of my innovations being adopted on a commercial scale. One particular project took me four years to work through all the experiments that were "apparent failures" to other people, but learning experiences for me. It was from these "apparent failures" that I really learned how to translate creative ideas into successful innovation. I am convinced that maintaining a "wanting to do it" attitude was what sustained me through this difficult period in my career.

Following this period of success, I entered into what I call the "dark period" of my career at DuPont. I had achieved successful innovation. The commercial processes were running much faster and making great financial return; but what was I to do next? I was in the situation that I referred to in Chapter 2: "Then when success was achieved, life returned to 'normal'; the business enterprise experienced great financial reward, and those that accomplished the success went their own way looking to contribute to another such project. The problem, of course, is there are few such projects because they are born out of either creativity or necessity. Creativity – when an enterprise happens upon an invention that offers the chance to grow organically. Necessity – when an enterprise is faced with survival."

I decided that I would create an opportunity for the business enterprise. I spent 5 years working to improve the quality of the processes for which I had increased the rates of production. I did this because I believed that future business success depended on improved quality. It was during this "dark period" that I came to appreciate how fleeting success is, and that accomplishing the next successful innovation is hard to come by. I struggled for those 5 years and ended up with nothing tangible to contribute to the business enterprise, hence a very "dark period." However I maintained my "wanting to do it attitude" and gained knowledge in terms of what did not work, which as fate would have it, would help me 10 years later formulate the creative concepts for my most challenging project. In fact, that knowledge gained served as constraints in the development of an "out-of-the-box" idea (see Chapter 7) for a totally new technology. The knowledge gained also served the business enterprise well when it was faced with survival immediately following my "dark period."

I followed the "dark period" in my career with several successful innovations that helped my business enterprise survive. Knowledge gained from the "dark period" played an important part in those innovations and transformed my career from average to where I become a DuPont Research Fellow. I was promoted to DuPont Fellow years later based on the creative concepts and innovations formulated from the "dark period." Again, maintaining a "wanting to do it" attitude sustained me during these difficult times and led to my ultimate successes.

I have worked with many colleagues over the years who did not have this attitude. They would readily accept that failing early was acceptable, or if they applied all the basic scientific principles they learned in school and things did not work out, then that was acceptable because they had approached the problem in the accepted way. I often wonder how many more great inventions the world would have if more people believed in maintaining a "wanting to do it" attitude.

Chapter 4

Determining That an Innovation Can Be Done

Anything can be done.
There are no show-stoppers.
Instead, the show never stops;
and failure is not an option.

View the world only in terms of
what it takes to achieve success.

It is more difficult to determine that something cannot be done than it is to determine that it can be done.

♦ It is impossible to prove that something cannot be done unless it violates the laws of physics.

♦ The successful innovator does not accept the concepts of "failing early" or that "show stoppers" exist.

♦ Successful innovators do not view the world in terms of success or failure because failure does not exist.

♦ Successful innovators adhere to the belief that anything can be done and are not discouraged when creative ideas do not work at first and require further improvement.

♦ Overcoming the frustration associated with converting creative ideas into successful innovations is a necessary part of the process.

Determining That an Innovation Can Be Done

How many times do you hear that "it cannot be done?" Yet the rate of the world's successful innovations (sometimes called progress) continues to accelerate. Obviously the innovators creating this progress do not adhere to the negative thinking associated with "it cannot be done." So what is it about these innovators that makes them successful? I submit that one basic characteristic of successful innovators is that they believe that it is more difficult to determine that something cannot be done than it is to determine that it can be done. Take some time to think about this statement. It is nearly impossible to prove that something cannot be done – unless it inherently violates the "laws of physics." Thus it follows that working to determine how to do something is the appropriate focus versus trying to find the so-called "show stoppers" or "failing early" so that resources can be directed to projects where success could be more probable.

The intent of this book is to convey techniques for dealing with this very issue – making an innovation successful, which is an enormously difficult task by any measure. This book may not be very useful to those who allow themselves to think that there are "show stoppers" or that "failing early" is an acceptable option. Obstacles will always be encountered and developing ideas and plans to overcome the obstacles is the job of the innovator. Firmly believing that anything can be done is at the core of succeeding. To even think that failure is an option negates the underlying condition of positive thinking that is required.

Thus the innovator must view the world only in terms of what it takes to achieve success. Success means getting the innovation to the commercial stage as soon as possible. However as pointed out in Chapter 1, the innovator must successfully navigate the Innovation Development Curve beforehand. To accomplish that, the innovator needs to determine that his/her innovation can be done in the shortest amount of time possible. There are two things that will help get to that stage fast:

1) Complete a formal QFD at the beginning of the project, and

2) Test a successful prototype or get positive customer feedback of a proof of concept sample as soon as possible.

These actions are discussed in Chapter 1 and are shown to shorten the timeline for the Innovation Development Curve, as well as reducing the risk of the innovation process for the funding enterprise. The importance of developing skill at completing a formal QFD cannot be understated. It is absolutely essential that the innovator has specifications for the product, service, or process that he/she is innovating. Creative concepts evolve from these specifications. Once the creative concepts are developed, then the innovator must strive for the simplest approach for making a successful prototype or proof of concept sample in the shortest amount of time. To do this, it is important that the innovator realize that perfection is not the goal. Getting positive feedback from the marketplace that validates the innovation is the goal. Once this positive feedback is obtained, then the innovator has determined that his/her innovation can be done.

Personal Experience

As one works to turn creativity into successful innovation, critical periods will be encountered when it may seem that nothing is working. During these periods it will be easy to think that "it cannot be done." Dealing with this frustration in a way that leads to success is a trait of the successful innovator. My personal experience dealing with this very issue is what led me to develop the "Laws" discussed herein. I have had to use every one of the "'Laws" to help me determine that innovations could be successfully achieved.

My undergraduate degree is in Aerospace Engineering and, as such, my favorite scientific topic has always been aerodynamics. From the first time I saw a rocket launch in the 1950s until today, aerodynamics has been my core technical interest. Throughout my career at DuPont, I was fortunate to have worked on many projects requiring this expertise. However, during the course of one of those projects, I encountered a problem that I thought might not be solvable and that I might be violating the laws of aerodynamics with my approach to solving the problem. As I struggled with this problem and experimented with many possible solutions – all of which did not work – I was ready many times to almost give up, but I kept asking myself "how do I know that there is not a solution?"

This was when it occurred to me that it was going to be more difficult for me to determine that the problem could not be solved than it was for me to solve it. What I needed was a successful prototype to determine that the problem could be solved. This happened in my career long before I became skilled in performing QFDs. Thus I did not have a formal set of criteria for what the prototype would have to do, or the constraints that could be relaxed as I sought possible "out-of-the-box" solutions. I was at the point of maximum risk on the Innovation Development Curve. Believe me this is a very uncomfortable place to be. You do not want to be there long! I was at the point where all innovators inevitably find themselves; and it is very, very lonely. I felt that things were spinning in an uncontrollable way. It was impossible to come up with a realistic idea that would lead to success. Nevertheless, I maintained a "wanting to do it" attitude and persevered in the quest to find a solution.

In Chapter 9, I suggest that the innovator use brainstorming to get back on track on the Innovation Development Curve. One of the key techniques of brainstorming is to develop new ideas based on relaxing the problem constraints. Innovators tend to seek perfection in the adaptation of their "brain children" and they will establish constraints which ensure perfect translation of their creative ideas into successful innovation. This is where I was in trying to solve this difficult aerodynamic problem; that is, imposing a constraint that prevented a practical solution.

An interesting facet about this experience is that I found a solution to this problem in a simulation laboratory well ahead of the struggle I experienced in trying to solve the problem live in a commercial production plant. The solution was such that I thought it would never be accepted in the commercial plant; thus I imposed a constraint that prevented the solution early in the innovation process. This critically important point is discussed in

Chapter 12; that is, how to avoid missing a path to success. I was fortunate in this circumstance to have a manager that advised me to relax my self-imposed constraint and suggested that I seek help in solving the problem. I accepted his advice and worked with team members to find a solution. We found a solution, and this experience reinforced my belief that anything can done.

Chapter 5

Letting Great Ideas Happen

Great ideas often come when least expected;
therefore, strive to get into a state of "flow"
instead of a state of stressful anticipation.

When things get difficult, do not try to force good ideas – just let them happen.

♦ Developing successful innovations from creative ideas leads to periods of great personal stress resulting from putting oneself at risk.

♦ Overcoming problems along the way requires even more good ideas which cannot be forced to occur.

♦ Getting into a state of "flow" often allows the best ideas to happen.

♦ A "state of flow" can be achieved by physically relaxing and letting your brain "flow" via positive visualization in 3D with color.

♦ Combining visualization with baseline knowledge of many diverse subjects improves the innovator's ability to develop great ideas.

Letting Great Ideas Happen

Once a QFD has been developed for a new product, service, or process it is time to figure out how to get to the successful prototype stage (or proof of concept sample stage) of the Innovation Development Curve. Creative ideas need to be developed that would accomplish the performance criteria required for a successful innovation. This chapter and the next 4 chapters discuss ways to do develop the great ideas required for success. The great ideas cannot be forced. They will come when least expected provided the innovator has in his/her mind the correct QFD requirements. However, having training and experience in several fields of endeavor can enhance the chance of developing great ideas Also the ability to visualize physical things in their three-dimensional aspects is a tremendous talent to possess (it can also be learned). Successful innovations in the twenty-first century will require blending and combining knowledge; therefore, combining visualization with baseline knowledge of many diverse subjects is a powerful, must have, addition to the innovator's tool kit.

When things get difficult on a project and nothing good seems to be happening, we all start struggling for the next good idea that will resolve things and set us back on the path to success. In other words, we try to force good ideas to occur. But it seems that the ideas just do not come! Perhaps this is because we sometimes get into a "funk" where our brains just do not work as normal, or we get irritable and it is hard to think straight, or we even start to blame our teammates. While this is intellectual in nature, it is also very akin to playing sports when we are not performing at our normal skill level. Since I am personally familiar with golf, it's like trying to force a good shot. It never works that way, at least not for me. I have found that I perform better at playing golf by just letting the good shots happen. This strategy works for scientific projects and any endeavor requiring the development of better ideas and concepts.

It is somewhat like asking the "man-on-the-street" question presented in Chapter 13. In that Chapter we learn to relax the constraints associated with a complicated situation and then to strive for the simplest approach possible. Here we want to relax our intensity for developing the next great idea and let our brains sort of float. Take the pressure off. Just let it happen. And it can happen anywhere – while walking around, while relaxing on the beach (my favorite place which works best for me), while daydreaming in a meeting at work, or who knows. Listen to your favorite music – especially songs that get you thinking positively about the success that awaits you. Close your eyes and visualize in three-dimensions and with everything in color. Let there be lots of light in your visualizations.

Once you have had some success using this approach, you will find that your chances of developing great ideas will improve. It takes practice. Success will build upon success. All I know is that it works for me, and I think you should try it. And by the way, you will know when you are "in the zone" and ready to let great ideas just happen!

Personal Experience

Experiencing that great ideas can happen when you least expect them is a very real phenomenon. I continue to be astounded at this incredible experience and how it occurs. As I have said, I think it takes a combination of knowledge of diverse subjects combined with all the attributes of a positive, creative innovator as discussed in this book. As I look back over my career and analyze the great ideas that led me to my most successful innovations, I realize that they came about in different ways; but having the commonalities of positive thinking and diverse knowledge. I cannot overly emphasize the value of visualization in 3D as the innovator imagines creative concepts to accomplish his/her innovation successfully. The talent to visualize in 3D will assist in the development of great ideas in all fields of endeavor; whether it is science, art, music, engineering, biology, chemistry, business, etc.

I have experienced the happenings of great ideas in many different ways. One way is to make sketches of your creative ideas. Make the sketches in 3D. Add color to differentiate the aspects of your concepts. Very often an initial sketch of the base concept will spark that great idea that the innovator is seeking. This happened to me as I was editing this section. I was working with a Venture Capital Firm to develop a new technology and I was drawing sketches for the patent application when the great idea occurred to me. I was totally flabbergasted when it happened.

Another way I have experienced the serendipity of occurrence of a great idea is when someone asks the "what if?" question. This happened to me once when I got a new boss and he requested to meet with me when I was going through some difficult times with a family member's health issues. It took a while for us to get together; but when we did, it was an amazing experience. He asked me if I thought it was possible to make a product in a totally different way from the present technology. He suggested the base concept, and I had to determine if it was possible. Of course to answer that question, I had to develop the great idea of how to do it. I came up with an idea that was somewhat "out-of-the-box;" but the point is that I would have never developed that idea without the "what if?" question.

Another way for great ideas to happen is to analyze data and get into a state of "flow." I can remember looking over a "rack-up" of some material pore size data and moisture vapor transmission rates one afternoon and letting my mind "float" as I contemplated the information. It was a beautiful, sunny afternoon and I was looking out the window at the grass and trees. During this time period I was gaining knowledge in areas adjacent to my core competency, which helped me formulate the great idea. I then realized that a new material functionality was possible.

While I have personally benefited from the approach of "just letting great ideas happen," I have found that the concept can make people nervous and perhaps less confident in your way of working. When I have mentioned the concept to some of my managers, I can see that they are uncomfortable with the approach. Managers like to have a "warm" feeling that their employees have things under control. Just the thought that an employee does not have the next step planned for his/her project is unacceptable. Again, I think that you need to have experienced some success with this approach to have confidence that it can work. To gain this experience, I would suggest that the innovator work to develop a back-up plan (see Chapter 16) derived from an idea developed by using this approach.

Chapter 6

Good Ideas Can Come From Anywhere

Keeping an open mind,
combined with open ears,
can lead to surprisingly good ideas.

Learn to listen – you just never know where a good idea will come from.

♦ Personal transformation from a "knowing person" to a "listening person" helps overcome the arrogance associated with one's own "great ideas" and allows for good ideas to come from somewhere else.

♦ Conversion of a creative idea into a working innovation requires multiple paths to success, and thus multiple good ideas which are best generated from multiple sources.

♦ Tapping into the global sources of information is easier than ever in the 21st century, thus the successful innovator must search everywhere for good ideas.

♦ Achieving a successful innovation is the desired result from a good idea – therefore, within the bound of ethical behavior, the source of the idea is irrelevant.

Good Ideas Can Come From Anywhere

Learning to listen is not a new type of advice. Many of the world's greatest thinkers have expressed the power of following this advice. However, in the scientific world where we are taught to strive to be "the expert" it's difficult to follow this advice. This is because if the innovator works in a large organization, achieving status as an "expert" is often associated with promotions and earning more money; thus the innovator tends to view himself/herself as someone who gives advice versus someone who listens to advice. However as the innovator becomes more skilled and accomplishes successful innovations, the transformation from a "knowing person" to a "listening person" will occur. This will allow great ideas to come from anywhere – from anyone – and at anytime. The innovator will always need to be on the alert for this random possibility and will find that his/her chances of success will increase.

Listening also goes along with being a team player. The 21st century engineering and science efforts have switched from individual effort to team effort, hence listening to team members from other scientific fields will be one major key to success. Ideas will have to be developed synergistically between our personal area of expertise and other team members' areas of expertise. Thus listening will be more important than ever.

Tapping into the global sources of information via the internet is another great way to get good ideas. While this is not listening per se, it is akin to listening. However, there is so much information available on-line that the challenge to the innovator is to sort out information that is relevant to his/her project. This will require some skill and seeking help and advice on how to develop that skill will greatly improve the innovator's ability to develop good ideas. An interesting phenomenon occurs when searching the internet, that is – information seems to be more believable when read as opposed to when heard. Chapter 14 discusses the perils of "totally believing what people tell you." This advice should be extended to information gathered from the internet. With this in mind, skill in searching for relevant information on the internet is essential for development of good ideas.

If the innovator's field is the arts, getting criticism and listening to that criticism will lead to improved art. Just as the senior technical innovator strives to be "the expert;" the artist strives for personal creativity at its highest level, which is manifested in his/her art. The innovator's creativity is very personal. Turning this creativity into a successful work of art takes the innovator down many paths and seeking advice along the way in the form of criticism is a smart thing to do. The successful innovator will act on the criticism and view this "listening" process as helpful to achieving his/her ultimate success.

In Chapter 16, I talk about developing multiple paths to success. This concept ties in with seeking to get good ideas from anywhere that you can. Use consultants and "outside experts" as sources of getting divergent ideas beyond those developed by yourself and your colleagues. Each day listen to someone else's ideas without judgment and keep a log (notebook) of all the ideas you encounter – especially yours!

It is a flawed notion that success is achieved by following some idealized path whereby one first researches all past work and then embarks on a well laid out plan based on the scientific method. Reality is that we start with a creative idea and perform some tests and experiments, then analyze the data, iterate with more tests, and maybe achieve some degree of positive results – enough to continue working on the project. Somewhere along the way, we blend in knowledge from outside sources including past work within our corporations.

Since good ideas can come from anywhere, in addition to listening, always be searching the past for relevant updated concepts to meet your current goals. Large corporations have an especially rich library of past work and it is incumbent upon researchers to be knowledgeable of what has been done. Do not hesitate to "borrow shamelessly" from your corporation's past work and apply it to what you are doing right now. It is not a matter of where the good idea came from, but rather a matter of accomplishing a successful innovation using that good idea. If the necessary idea lies outside your corporation, then license it or form a joint venture. Do whatever it takes to make your project successful, of course within the bounds of professional and business ethics.

Personal Experience

There came a point in my career in which I flipped from being a "knowing person" to a "listening person." This came about as I got comfortable with my career – feeling that I had accomplished much and no longer had anything to prove – in other words, it came about as a result of success. Once you "flip" over to being a listener, I think that you will enjoy listening more than talking and you will find that your level of success will improve.

I have found that few of the people working in large organizations take time to review the past work of their colleagues when assigned to a new project. The tendency is to jump in and start producing results as soon as possible. This probably goes back to the innovator wanting to be "the expert" and showing original results that can be attributed solely to him/her. But as the innovator matures and achieves some success, the value of researching past work becomes a more important part of his/her toolkit. One of my colleagues at DuPont had a saying "you can save 6 months in the lab by spending 4 hours in the library!" He practiced what he preached and was very successful at accomplishing his projects. I think that following his own advice was a significant contributor to his success.

In my career at DuPont, I borrowed many ideas and concepts from engineers and scientists that had previously worked in my organization. Large organizations fund many projects, and as business conditions change with time the results may be simply "put on the shelf." Two things are very important for the organization to gain value from this "tabled" work: 1) the innovators must write reports and archive them in the corporation's library, and 2) the successful innovator must research these reports and become knowledgeable of the past work pertaining to his/her creative concepts. It took me some time in my career before I realized the value of researching my corporation's past knowledge, and then dialing that knowledge back into my work. I had one experience in which I was able to apply past knowledge to a project requiring altering a product's mechanical properties. The project was a success, and what was amazing was that the organization credited me with the innovation! Although I always referenced where I got the basic information for the innovation, the innovation always bore my name because I was the one that pushed it through to successful conclusion.

I had another interesting experience in which I borrowed past knowledge, developed a process improvement, and verified that it worked in commercial operation; only to have business conditions change leading to tabling of the innovation. In that case, there was a double tabling of the basic knowledge. Because of the archiving of the knowledge and subsequent innovation, the business organization has an innovation "on the shelf" whenever the need arises. This leads to an important point: whenever a new manager or senior scientist enters an existing organization, he/she should "rack up" all innovations that are sitting "on the shelf" and look to extract value for the funding organization.

Chapter 7

Getting Truly "Out-of-the-Box"

Ideas subjected to the constraints of reality,

and combined with experience,

lead to successful thinking

outside the so-called "box."

Successful "out-of-the-box" thinking requires – first having been "in-the-box."

♦ "Out-of-the-box" ideas that have the best chance of conversion to successful innovations are developed from practical thinking grounded in the reality of experience, i.e., having been "in-the-box."

♦ Practice all known techniques for stretch thinking while developing "out-of-the-box" ideas – then impose realistic constraints on the best ideas.

♦ Practice other "Laws of Successful Innovation and Creativity" described herein to develop good "out-of-the-box" ideas; especially, those describing how to let great ideas happen and learning to listen.

♦ Be prepared to put your ideas, and yourself, at risk (criticism, etc.) in order to pursue "out-of-the-box" ideas.

Getting Truly "Out-of-the-Box"

How many times have you heard someone say "let's get out-of-the-box in our thinking?" Sounds like it could be easy to do. Just think more broadly, more boldly. Just think beyond what you would ordinarily do. Just do some stretch thinking. No problem – just remember, it's easy.

But we want to successfully get "out-of-the-box." We do not want to just develop some irrelevant ideas and say that we have developed some "out-of-the-box" ideas. I firmly believe that to accomplish this, you first have to "have been in the box." By this, I mean you have to have realistic experience working in the field of endeavor in which you are trying to develop "out-of-the-box" ideas. The realistic experience of "having been in the box" grounds your thinking in a practical way. It puts constraints on your thinking in a positive way. You still have to stretch your thinking, but within some realistic limits. With these limits in mind, practice all known creative techniques for brainstorming and idea generation. There are many techniques and they can easily be found in the literature. The trick is to practice divergent thinking while imposing realistic constraints.

As discussed in the second chapter of this book, a successful innovator will always be at risk. Pursuing "out-of-the-box" ideas will especially put you at risk. The first reaction of many of us is to look unfavorably upon a new idea – it just seems to be human behavior. Therefore, a truly "out-of-the-box" idea will garner stiff critique from colleagues and managers. With this difficulty in mind, it's essential that realistic constraints be imposed on your ideas before taking action to pursue work on them.

Personal Experience

I have been asked many times "how did you come up with that idea?" or "where did that concept come from?" Most of the time I have answered that it just occurred to me. But upon further reflection, during the course of writing this book, I realized that many skills went into development of a truly "out-of-the-box" idea. The idea did not come about from an "out of the blue" occurrence, or from pure circumstance. I also have come to believe that those skills can be learned. Next I present the most important skills required for getting truly "out-of-the-box."

Skills Required to Get Truly "Out-of-the Box"

1) *Practical Experience*
    The most basic skill required is to have practical experience in the field of endeavor of the innovation. I had years of experience to draw upon, which helped me develop creative ideas and impose practical constraints on those ideas.

2) *Expertise in Many Fields*
    Great "out-of-the-box" ideas usually involve multiple technologies, or fields of endeavor. I developed expertise in many fields relevant to my core focus of work; and

was able to use that knowledge, along with practical experience, to impose constraints on divergent ideas.

3) *Use of Knowledgeable Colleagues*
As mentioned previously, at DuPont there were many talented and knowledgeable engineers and scientists. I was able to use those colleagues for critical reviews of my ideas, and for improvements upon those ideas, prior to embarking too far along the Innovation Development Curves.

4) *Use of Rack-Ups*
As discussed in Chapter 5, learning how to do a succinct "rack-up" of data and relevant information is essential to the development of a great idea. Once I learned how to do simple rack-ups to lay out data, I developed many "out-of-the-box" ideas using this technique.

5) *Strive for Simplicity*
Great "out-of-the-box" ideas do not have to be complicated; in fact, they should be as simple as possible. Once you have conceived of an idea, try to simplify it. Use as much known technology as possible. Over the years, I learned that simplicity is more important than complexity and that principle has contributed much to my success.

6) *Learn to Practice the Techniques Presented in this Book*
The more important techniques presented in this book for helping to develop "out-of-the-box" ideas are:

a) striving for the simplest approach, Chapter 13
b) letting great ideas happen, Chapter 5
c) believing that good ideas can come from anywhere, Chapter 6
d) striving for creative ideas at a higher level, Chapter 19

7) *Become Comfortable with Putting Ideas at Risk*
Subjecting your ideas to criticism, and benefiting from that criticism, is part of the process of developing great ideas. The innovator must become comfortable with this approach. I never had an aversion to putting my ideas and my career at risk. Thus, I think that is probably the most important skill for successful innovation.

All these skills were used to develop an "out-of-the-box" idea for my most ambitious project. I can especially remember calling a meeting in which I requested critical review of the basic idea by several of my knowledgeable colleagues. I proceeded ahead with the QFD for the innovation following that meeting. While this was an incredibly complicated technological innovation, I strived for simplicity using as much proven technology as possible. I also recruited team members based on their expertise and willingness to take career risk by working on a difficult project where success was not assured.

Chapter 8

Doing Your Best Work When Things Look the Bleakest

The greatest successes arise from
the times of the greatest darkness.

Do your best work when things look the bleakest.

♦ Turning a creative idea into a successful innovation is an extremely difficult thing to accomplish – very few people in history have been capable of doing this.

♦ The perseverance required to be successful sometimes leads to long periods of frustration, which in turn leads to a "personal feeling of always being down."

♦ Developing the skill to perform analysis with a simple, high level rack-up of the project's status will enable focus on the right things to work on.

♦ Realizing that success will require doing your absolute best work at this time should lead to a remarkable state of calm and reassurance.

♦ In fact, one of life's greatest experiences occurs when success is achieved after a long period of bleakness and struggle.

Doing Your Best Work When Things Look the Bleakest

Research work is said to be > 99 % perspiration. I would say that based on my experiences it is > 99 % frustration. It has to be this way if you are pushing the limits of your development, or "pushing the envelope," as some like to say. Inevitably, there will be times when things look so bad and bleak that you will want to give up. This is human. During such times, one thing that has worked well for me is to keep saying to myself "this is the time when I have to do my absolute best work." This very thought has a comforting effect and enables the mind to focus back on the problem at hand as opposed to dwelling on the negative thought that failure might be a possibility.

Doing your best work during a time of great frustration and personal stress requires application of many of the techniques, or "Laws," discussed in this book. In addition, a functional skill that is absolutely required for you to do your best work is to be able to succinctly rack-up data and information. By this, I mean the skill to render a situation down to its most basic elements and facts and develop a simple way to display the data and information for interpretation. With the advent of the personal computer and statistical design packages, this skill seems somewhat "old fashioned" I suppose, but I have used it many times with good success.

Very few people can deal with an almost constant state of frustration and still be able to do great work. However, once you have achieved a successful innovation you will realize the necessity of being able to deal with frustration as part of the struggle for ultimate success. In fact, achieving success after a long period of bleakness and struggle is one of life's most extraordinary experiences. Experience this a couple of times and you will be addicted to successful innovation!

Personal Experience

Perhaps the bleakest period of my professional career occurred as I was scaling up a process to higher rates of production and encountered an unexpected difficulty just as the project was being commercialized. In spite of conducting several successful full-scale commercial runs of the new process, a product defect showed up when the plant was converted. This defect had never been encountered before, so no one had any experience and advice on how to solve the problem. I went through all the usual techniques of trying to determine what was different versus the successful trial runs, and came up empty-handed. I changed many process settings, only to find out that they were not as important as was thought. I had a basic hunch that the problem was electrical in nature and associated with high voltage physics. I finally spent many days reviewing past research in this area and developed a hypothesis for the cause of the problem.

All during this time, I felt very down and was under a great deal of stress and did not know if the hypothesis that I had developed was the correct one. Things looked very bleak. In times like this, there is a great tendency to do something directed at a solution to the problem whether it is grounded in sound thinking or not.

In other words, just do something because it looks like you are doing something in the eyes of your business associates. I had to resist this tendency and take time away from the daily grind to review the past research work – thus, I had to do my best work just when things looked the bleakest.

After about a month of struggle, I was able to design a solution to the defect problem based on my hypothesis for the cause. Being able to deal with the frustration associated with this unexpected problem enabled me to be successful in finding a solution. After this period, my career was never the same again because I gained the confidence necessary to deal with any situation and realized that overcoming frustration is part of being a successful innovator. When I recall the perseverance that it took to make this project successful, I realize that it is one of my life's greatest experiences.

Chapter 9

Brainstorming to Get Back on Track

Individual arrogance must give way to the wisdom of seeking help via brainstorming.

Use Brainstorming as a Method to Get Back on the Innovation Development Curve.

♦ The Innovation Development Curve is not a smooth function, but rather a jagged function the innovator will have to struggle with to stay on track.

♦ Brainstorming is an effective technique for supplying the innovator with ideas and concepts to assist in keeping the innovation on track, or to help the innovator get back on track.

♦ The innovator will benefit the most from a brainstorming session by having it well designed and led by a trained leader.

♦ Participants must be chosen who are diverse in their experience and background, and there must be at least one expert in each technology area encompassed by the innovation.

♦ The output of the session must be acted upon by the innovator, and the participants should reconvene and assess the effectiveness of the innovator's actions.

Brainstorming to Get Back on Track

Conversion of creativity into successful innovation is not a well defined path or experience. The Innovation Development Curve depicted as a smooth function in Figure 1 is just that – a depiction of reality. As said previously, the innovator will have to do many things for ultimate success, and among these is to "stay on track." Staying on track means that the innovator has the feeling of continuous momentum as work proceeds. Even the appearance of staying on track is very important, especially when the innovator is working in a large corporation or organization.

Despite the best efforts of the innovator, many development projects will reach a point where the feeling of being off track occurs. Several chapters of this book are devoted to generating ideas and concepts when needed, but another well known technique that can help the innovator get back on track is brainstorming. But the innovator must realize that he/she needs help and then let go of his/her individual arrogance and ask for help. The term arrogance is used here because innovators are typically very intelligent people and a certain individual arrogance comes with that personal characteristic. However, as the innovator achieves success and gains wisdom, it becomes easier to ask for help. The great innovators know that ultimate project success is the goal, and therefore they will use whatever techniques can help them.

For brainstorming to have a good chance of being helpful, certain principles should be followed; the most important of which are:

1) the meeting must be conducted by a trained leader, and 2) a diverse group of participants in terms of expertise, experience and background must be invited. There must be at least one expert in each of the technology areas involved. And most importantly, the innovator must act on the output of the meeting. A suggested outline for an effective brainstorming session is presented next.

Outline of an Effective Brainstorming Meeting
(How to Get Back on the Innovation Development Curve)

1) *Develop the problem statement*
   a) Review project functional requirements, i.e., QFD
   b) Rack-up relevant data and trends
   c) Each participant presents an assessment of their problem statement
   d) Define a consensus problem statement

The most important thing to do for a good brainstorming session is to make sure that all participants have a clear understanding of the problem statement. Believe it or not, sometimes the innovator may not have a clear understanding of his/her own problem. Or as he/she proceeds along the Innovation Development Curve, things change in terms of what can be accomplished, and the original project goal (or problem statement) gets shifted. The purpose of the brainstorming session is to get back on track, and reaffirming the project goal with all its QFD requirements is the first thing to do.

2) *Define the problem constraints*

    a) Led by group leader and experts in the area

The constraints imposed by the innovator should be analyzed to make sure that they are understood by all. Constraints are the things that the innovator eliminates as possible solutions to the problem statement. They could also be things that limit the application of a possible solution. In Chapter 4, I discussed how this happened to me once; that is, I imposed a constraint that prevented me from finding a solution to my problem. And when the constraint was relaxed, the problem was readily solved by a new approach made possible by that relaxation.

3) *Relax the problem constraints*

    a) Participants develop ideas
    b) Participants present their ideas to the group

Relaxing the problem constraints can lead to new ideas for solving the problem statement. It is important that all participants understand what constraints mean and how to relax them based on the technologies involved in the innovation.

4) *Each participant develops an explanation of the problem for the "man-on-the-street"*

    a) Each participant presents their explanation to the group and how their "man-on-the-street" would solve the problem statement

Chapter 13 describes the "man-on-the-street" approach as being able to summarize all key complexities of a desired innovation into a simple, easy to understand problem statement; and then being able to explain this statement to someone not familiar with the problem at hand. The participant needs to understand this concept in order to develop conceivable solutions for their "man-on-the-street." The session leader must make sure that the participants are properly instructed.

5) *Each participant develops an idea for the simplest thing that can be done*
    a) Each participant presents their idea to the group
Striving for simplicity means that the participants should use the minimum complexity as they develop their possible solutions to the problem statement.

6) *Each participant develops an "out-of-the-box" idea*
    a) Each participant presents their idea to the group
"Out-of-the-box" ideas are best developed after understanding the practical constraints of the problem statement from an expert in the field of the innovation to be developed. The session leader should then guide the participants through the various techniques for stretch thinking as they develop their idea.

7) *Each participant develops a back-up plan*
    a) Each participant presents their back-up plan to the group
Chapter 16 discusses the value of having a back-up plan(s) to attaining successful innovation. An alternate path to success may be found by having the participants think of how they would approach solving the problem statement in a different way.

8) *Determine if the project can be approached in terms of steps*
   a) Group discussion
   b) Determine the steps to be taken if the project can be approached in steps

   Chapter 15 discusses how complex innovations can be achieved in steps. The session leader will lead the participants in a group analysis of the problem statement to determine if breaking the innovation into definitive smaller work streams (steps) is possible. If the participants determine that the problem statement can be approached in steps, the innovator will be assigned the task of working up a back-up plan using a step approach. This will be a path forward item for the innovator.

9) *Visualize project success – define what it looks like*
   a) Determine if anything can be compromised and look for application of the 80-20 rule

   The session leader will get group consensus on the vision for project success:
   − Will it meet the problem statement QFDs?
   − Will it be accomplished on time?
   − If the answer to either of these questions is no, then the session leader will have the group determine if the 80-20 rule can be applied to see if there is value in what has been accomplished so far.

10) *Document the output from the meeting and develop the path forward for the innovator*

    The outcome of the brainstorming session should be documented by the session leader, not the innovator. This is to eliminate bias and make sure that a proper path forward is defined aimed only at achieving total or partial project success.

11) *Reconvene the group and assess the innovator's actions*
The session leader should reconvene the group in 3 months to assess the innovator's progress on the path forward items. At that time, a new path forward may be developed and the cycle repeated.

Personal Experience

Over the years I have participated in many brainstorming sessions, most of which have not yielded a lot of value to the ongoing innovation development. On the contrary, the QFD (see the Definitions section) sessions associated with the Concurrent Engineering (CE), or CE (see Definitions section), method seem to have yielded new ideas that have been valuable. I designed the brainstorming session presented above to take advantage of what the QFD and CE methods offer. I also used my personal experiences combined with key techniques described in this book.

A key to successful brainstorming is for all participants to listen (see Chapter 6) to the ideas and opinions of the other participants. This must be worked into the design of the session and enforced by the leader of the session. The participants need to be flexible enough to change their own opinions after listening to others and then upgrade those personal opinions into improved ideas and concepts.

Having participants present from all aspects of the innovation is also critical to a successful brainstorming session. I can recall conducting a design session relating to a QFD for a new innovative fiber spinning assembly and making sure that a certain technology was represented. The individual involved was somewhat bored all day until a particular aspect of the design was discussed which required his expertise – then he contributed an idea that was ultimately incorporated into the final design and had a major impact on its commercial success.

In addition to conducting brainstorming sessions when the project needs to get back on track, I would also propose a brainstorming session when things were going very well in order to take the innovation to a higher level (see Chapter 19). This is an exciting new concept. Most innovators are so thankful to achieve success that they just want to move on, but there may be adjacent or lateral innovations that could flow from the primary innovation. When innovators are in a state of achieving success, their creativity will be at its highest level and it is therefore a great time to develop new ideas.

Chapter 10

Learning from Ideas That Do Not Work

There are no bad ideas, just ideas that need to be improved upon to become better ideas.

Learn more from ideas that do not work than you learn from ideas that do work.

◆ Nothing is easy – only the novice thinks that things work the first time around.

◆ Expect that learning from ideas that do not work is part of the process of successful innovation.

◆ The period of greatest progress is made by analyzing results from apparently failed experiments.

◆ The phenomenon of serendipity often occurs as the innovator strives for better ideas.

Learning From Ideas That Do Not Work

The successful innovator realizes that a creative idea seldom works as envisioned the first time around and that iteration is a part of the process. Unfortunately, it has become easy for some people and organizations to get to where this basic reality is overlooked. The modern business enterprise seems to have little patience for the process of iteration because it takes time, and of course time is viewed as money. Nevertheless, the innovator must persevere and learn from things that do not work and continue the iterative process until success is achieved.

You put enoromous effort into designing and executing experiments and tests, only to get results that you did not expect, and these are usually disappointing. However, the successful innovator learns from experience that analyzing the results of experiments that do not work is one of the most important things that he/she can do. You have to overcome the disappointment and put in the long hours analyzing the results in very intricate detail. This is when you learn the most! But I have found that this is very, very difficult to do all the time, in spite of firmly knowing that it is required for success.

The term serendipity is often used to describe unexpected results that lead to new and useful findings. The phenomenon of serendipity can certainly occur as the result of experiments that have apparently failed. Thus, continually telling yourself to learn more from ideas that do not work than you learn from ideas that do work is helpful motivation for the successful innovator.

Since the success rate for innovations is very low, say <10%, this is especially good advice for innovators that are just beginning their career.

Personal Experience

I have found that too many researchers are quick to draw conclusions so that they can quickly design their next experiment. That way, there is the feeling that progress is being made and the project is moving forward. Large organizations like to see their employees in "motion" because it means the employees are focused on the organization's goals. However, this can be false "motion" unless the researchers take time to analyze results, then design and execute well planned experiments. My experience has been that it takes much longer to evaluate the results of experiments than it takes to design and execute experiments. If the innovator develops art works, this would be like producing too many poor works of art versus a few quality art works.

I have encountered this situation over and over in my career. It just seems difficult for us to take the time up front. The tendency to show activity prevails. As I was completing this book, I was asked to consult on a very difficult problem that a major corporation was having and immediately I could tell that they were focusing on activity as opposed to developing a rational way to solve the problem. The personnel involved had no idea how to do a "rack-up" of their existing knowledge. They were embarking on an elaborate statistically designed experimental plan. I did a simply rack-up of their existing knowledge and showed them how to radically reduce the number of variables to test. Of course, doing a professional "rack-up" requires diligence and access to existing knowledge; which has to be properly searched, scrutinized, and summarized in a form that a "cave man" could understand. This takes time up front, and I have found that few people can and will make the required effort.

One of my first encounters with learning from apparently failed experiments occurred when I started working on my Ph.D. dissertation. One of my advisors asked me to program an analog computer to predict and monitor the amplitude responses from two nonlinearly coupled modes of motion. I did this and got an unexpected result which my advisor thought was impossible and he suggested that I reprogram the equations and "get it right this time." As any graduate student would do, I followed his instructions; however, I got the same result, which was that energy would unexpectedly shift back-and-forth between the modes of oscillation. This result, which came from an apparent failed experiment, formed the basis of my Ph.D. dissertation* and led to more than thirty years of successful research into nonlinear ship motions by my advisors.

* "Nonlinear Ship Motions in Regular Waves," Ph.D. Dissertation, Virginia Polytechnic Institute and State University, Larry R. Marshall, March, 1974.

Chapter 11

Practicing Compromise

Perfect conversion of creative ideas
into successful innovations does not exist.

Successful innovation is best accomplished with partial realization of great ideas; therefore, practice compromise, declare victory, and move on.

♦ In business and in the marketplace, partial realization of a creative idea is a successful innovation.

♦ Do not expect to perfectly convert creative ideas into innovations, instead practice the 80-20 rule and strive to attain 80% of the perfect result by using only 20% of the effort envisioned to achieve the perfect result.

♦ Apply the 80-20 rule by practicing compromise and not trying to attain technical perfection.

♦ The successful innovator knows that creative ideas cannot be perfectly converted into reality; thus, once business success is attained, accept this principle and move on to your next project.

Practicing Compromise

Practicing compromise is a very powerful innovation technique because it can lead to faster adaptation of your creative ideas and work. I think the basic thought is that success means getting as much value as possible from our innovations, which in turn means getting the innovation into the marketplace as fast as possible. To improve speed, we have to realize that getting 80% application of a great idea is very valuable. We do not have to get everything that is theoretically possible to have a successful innovation! Again, our education process teaches us to always find "the solution" or "the answer." But maybe an answer that is 80% correct is a very good one, if it means value in the marketplace. This is the 80-20 rule (see Definitions at the beginning of this book).

It is difficult for innovators to practice compromise because their creations are their "babies" and they have an intense determination to make them successful in the form that they were conceived. At the start of the innovation development cycle, compromise is not an acceptable thought. But as risk increases, the successful innovator will embrace compromise and use this technique as one of his/her most basic concepts for getting innovations accomplished.

I often tell my colleagues that innovative developments are never perfectly finished. So they shouldn't worry about it. As one of my managers used to say "extract value as soon as you can, declare victory, and move on."

Personal Experience

I first learned the value of this "Law" when working on an aerodynamic device. Engineering design theory told me that such a device should be designed like those of the space shuttle. Until I started working on this problem, the incumbent design had a geometrical shape that significantly departed from that of the space shuttle and engineering design theory. I applied the engineering design theory and developed a new device based on that theory. The final design matched the shape used on the space shuttle. I tested the device in the lab and it worked as envisioned. All seemed well until I tested the new device in the commercial plant. To my chagrin, the newly designed device made a defect which precluded its commercial success.

I will never forget driving home on a Friday night when I had the new devices running in the commercial plant. I was very proud of the job I had done and was very, very excited. Then I got the call saying that my devices were producing a defect. It was my first major plant trial at a DuPont commercial facility and it was my "baby." I was totally devastated. When I went into the plant that night and saw the defect first hand, I knew that my life would never be the same again because it taught me just how difficult successful innovation was going to be. I learned that innovation is not for those who are naïve and that one's creations must be tested in the real world of commercial operation. For the innovator in the art world, this means that one's works of art must withstand the tests of both time and criticism. The great works of art have to be accepted and great innovations have to really work.

Following the plant trial that did not work, I spent a very long time experimenting with various device designs to eliminate the defects. I was unsuccessful. Then my boss, who was a very experienced scientist, gave me the secret to success – practice compromise. I made a design which incorporated the essential elements of engineering design theory with a key element of the incumbent design. This compromised design worked well enough to be of value in the marketplace. And it did not produce the defects which had precluded application of the theoretically perfect design. This was my first major commercial innovation and it came about as a result of compromise. It taught me that practicing compromise is a very powerful technique for achieving successful innovation.

Chapter 12

Avoiding Missing a Path to Success

A path to success always exists and the
successful innovator must navigate
them all and never give up.

An innovator's greatest fear
should be – missing a path to success.

◆ The unyielding view that anything can be accomplished is at the heart of successful innovation and creativity; therefore, all paths that could lead to success must be taken.

◆ Taking multiple paths to success means that all ideas must be explored and the innovator should not be discouraged when some paths are found to be dead-ends.

◆ Everything imaginable must be explored to find a path to success; especially asking for help and listening to advice.

◆ Since failure does not exist, the innovator must know that a successful path does exist; hence, fear of missing the successful path should serve as a powerful motivator.

Avoiding Missing a Path to Success

I often wonder how many great inventions have been "left on the table" so-to-speak. In other words, the would-be inventor missed a path to success. Perhaps he or she simply tired of the seemingly endless effort required for success. Perhaps the inventor did not just let that last great idea happen as discussed in Chapter 5. Perhaps the inventor did not develop multiple paths to success as discussed in Chapter 16. Perhaps a "personal" discussion with a "man-on-the-street" would have been all that was needed as discussed in Chapter 13. This is the time when you have to say to yourself that it is more difficult to determine that something cannot be done than it is to determine that something can be done as discussed in Chapter 4. You have to maintain the drive and intensity to follow all leads and "wrestle them to the ground" in order to determine their merit and value to your project's success. This is very difficult to do and perhaps the most difficult thing to do. Maintaining an optimistic attitude when you are struggling requires great determination. Yet you absolutely have to do it if you have any chance of being successful at innovation and creativity. You just never know when serendipity will play a part and more or less hand you a solution or present a new opportunity that you have not planned on or considered. This is what Edison probably meant when he said "success is 1% inspiration and 99% perspiration." This is where all of the techniques presented in this book, or "Laws," sort of come together; that is: having an open mind, listening, never thinking a negative thought, maintaining that anything can be accomplished, getting truly "out-of-the-box," talking things over with your "men-on-the-street," having multiple back-up plans, thinking in the simplest possible terms, ...

Personal Experience

There was a time in my career when I did not understand the value of asking for help. I was trained to always find an answer to engineering problems as an individual. Naturally, that was how I approached the projects that I was assigned early in my career. Later on I did learn the value of asking for help when things got difficult on a project and it forged my attitude that a path to success can always be found. A good example of this happened when I was trying to find a way to solve a very difficult aerodynamic problem. I remember trying experiment after experiment only to end up in the same place – too many severe turbulent interactions. This went on for a very long time and with each new experiment I thought that success would follow. Finally, I was assigned a new manager and he relaxed the constraints which I was imposing to solve the problem; hence opening up new possibilities. He said he understood that something besides what I was doing was required. I listened to his advice about trying other approaches based on his experience. This led to a contract at a university where we did fundamental experiments to better understand the phenomena involved. Based on a new approach resulting from the work at the university, we were able to solve the problem and implement a solution (credit also goes to DuPont's Michael Davis). If I had just given up and not continued to pursue another path to success, then this process would not exist.

From this personal experience, I developed the guidance presented in Chapter 16. In that chapter I talk about developing multiple paths to success. The fear of missing a path to success, therefore, has led me to the firm belief that you must have as many back-up plans as you can envision and you have to go down each one searching for the one that will enable you to be successful. Having the fortitude to endure the effort, time, and frustration associated with "avoiding missing a path to success" is what separates the successful innovator from the ones who are not successful.

Chapter 13

Striving for the Simplest Approach

The ability to render a difficult problem into its absolute simplest form leads to much success.

Strive for the simplest approach by asking "what would a 'man-on-the-street' think and do when faced with this difficult situation?"

♦ Successful innovation involves complex interactions between science, marketing, business systems, and the skill of the innovator.

♦ However, innovation at its highest level results from simplicity.

♦ It is necessary to be able to summarize all the key complexities into a very simple problem statement, and then be able to express this statement to someone not familiar with the problem at hand – the so-called "man on-the-street."

♦ It is amazing how well this very simple approach can work and lead the innovator to the use of minimum complexity.

♦ Developing skill to "rack-up" only the essential "big picture" data for analysis will enhance the innovator's chance for success.

I credit the phrase "man-on-the-street" to The Steve Allen Show of the 1950s, which was a favorite TV show of mine as I grew up.

Striving for the Simplest Approach

It is easy to get trapped into thinking that the highest level of scientific work requires an equally high level of approach. In other words, complexity requires complexity. I think that this line of thinking goes back to our training in engineering and science where we are taught complicated differential equations and mathematics as tools to help us find solutions to very complicated problems. Using these tools is certainly necessary and required in general, however, there is another dimension to solving complicated problems and that takes the form of creative thinking which strives for the simplest approach. I have used this line of thinking very successfully many times in my career.

As we know, Einstein spent his last 30 years searching for a "unified field theory" which would explain all physical phenomena in a set of "simple" equations that would unify relativity theory with quantum theory. Thus the most noted scientist of the twentieth century sought the simplest approach when working on the most complicated problem ever to face mankind. There is a lesson to be learned here and I think that is: successful innovation, at its highest level, is based on simplicity. And in engineering terms, simple things are the things that will work the best. Use only as much complexity as is needed.

When faced with an incredibly difficult situation or problem, there is an approach that I use that has worked remarkably well for me many times; and that is to ask myself, "What would a 'man-on-the-street' think or do?" You have to imagine presenting the problem to the "man-on-the-street" in its absolute simplest form without all the constraining information that exists. This constraining information often "blinds" us to an obvious solution. It is the process of doing this in your mind that seems to liberate your thinking into patterns that are different than usual. That is, different from those thought patterns that occur when you also dial all the constraints into the thinking process. Creative ideas resulting from the new thought pattern seem to just "pop up at any time." They cannot be forced. I have found that they just happen on their own.

Personal Experience

I had a project in which the computer simulations of a material under strain predicted that we should use a "simulating" material in our prototype which was less rigid than what we were planning to use commercially. We spent a year experimenting with various "simulating" materials and none of them were satisfactory. While walking on the beach during my vacation, I asked myself this question: "What would a man-on-the-street do when presented with this situation?" In other words, take away the constraints imposed by the computer modeling and the advice of the consulting engineers. The absolute first thing that popped into my mind was – try using the stiffer material that we were planning to use commercially! We put the stiffer material on the prototype and it worked perfectly well. I went away from that experience more resolute than ever to always strive for the simplest approach.

Another technique that flows from this line of thinking is what is called a "rack-up." A "rack-up" is where only the essential data are summarized, i.e., the big picture information. I have found that very few people can do this. I think the reason is that most people rely only on their technical training and employ computers and statistical analysis packages to analyze data. But I also think there is another dimension to solving very complicated problems that relies on seeking simplicity and a good "rack-up" can provide valuable insight to compliment the analysis packages available to engineers.

Chapter 14

Avoiding Negative Thoughts

Positive thinking leads to creativity,
therefore avoiding negative thoughts
is an essential part of being a
successful innovator.

Avoid thinking negative thoughts and never totally believe what people tell you.

♦ Pursue successful innovations with the conviction that anything can be accomplished – negative thoughts are not a part of the process.

♦ Always approach innovation and creativity as if the glass is half full – negative thinkers are not creative thinkers.

♦ Question the observations and opinions of others – do not totally believe them – successful innovators develop their own baseline information upon which to base their creative ideas.

♦ Avoiding negative thoughts may be the single most distinguishing characteristic of the creative thinker and successful innovator.

Avoiding Negative Thoughts

We have all heard the old saying that positive thinkers always see the glass as half full while the negative thinkers see the glass as half empty. I have always seen the glass as half full and that has been a major part of my success as an engineer. I come from the point of view that anything can be accomplished. There is always a path to success. You just have to find it. But in order to find it, you have to firmly believe that it exists. If you think negatively by thinking that perhaps there is not a way to accomplishing your goal, then I think that you are already headed down the proverbial primrose path.

I know that complicated developments will lead to times when despair will tend to overcome the innovator. I have been there. As discussed in Chapter 8 this is when you have to do your best work. I have seen things developed that I thought might not happen, and this has reinforced my assertion that you must always proceed with the conviction that anything can be accomplished. To do your best work you cannot think negative thoughts. Always remember that your absolute best work will occur only when you think your best positive thoughts.

However, while we certainly want to think positively, how do we avoid negative thoughts from creeping in? A technique that works for me, when I sense that I am starting to go down that path to negative thinking, is to make myself ...Stop... Regroup... and Focus on something positive that I have going on. This is where it is so valuable to have multiple back-up plans and multiple side projects all going on simultaneously. The more the better, as long as you can manage them all. Just the mental refocusing on the other things will take you back to a positive frame of mind. Hopefully, this process will re-energize you when you go back to the activity that was starting to bring about the negative thinking and allow positive thoughts to emerge again.

Sometimes the opinions of others can be a source of, and lead to, negative thinking. I think that the right thing to do is – not totally believe all the opinions that are offered on a problem or project. The successful innovator must question the sources of information and work to make sure that the information used is unbiased. A technique that is very useful is to develop the information for writing a white paper on the subject at hand. White papers are meant to be objective in their descriptions and assessments. Compiling the information and organizing it, as if you are writing a white paper, ensures an unbiased assessment from which the innovator can develop the right kind of thoughts leading to rational thinking.

Personal Experience

As I have discussed many times in this book, positive thinking has been at the core of my career as an engineer and innovator. Now that I have moved on to the later phase of my career and life, I realize that this is what has sustained me and is a core value in my life. In the final analysis, it may be the single most distinguishing characteristic of the successful innovator and the creative thinker. Therefore, always be looking to turn negative thinking into something positive.

I recall a situation where a highly complicated new process was being developed to replace an incumbent one that was being phased out. My job was to develop whatever technology was required to insure that the products made using the new process were a match with the products from the process being phased out. Initially the product properties of the new process did not match those of the incumbent process. There was a lot of negative thinking in the organization because a situation like this had not been encountered before and no one knew what to do. The stakes were high – our customers demanded the product properties of the incumbent process, and if the new process could not deliver, then a high volume of sales would be lost to competitors. When faced with situations like this, I have found that a good practice is to design and conduct experiments that "bound-the-problem." By this I mean extend the range of past knowledge with some "out-of-the-box" tests. (Of course, the "out-of-the-box" tests need to adhere to the guidance presented in Chapter 7.) As a result of this approach, I was able to not only match the product properties required for conversion to the new process, but also to extend the product functionality of the new process far beyond that of the incumbent process.

While I was finishing this book, I encountered a situation as a consultant to the R&D organization of a major corporation in which a result was being obtained in the research laboratory that did not match the commercial experience. As I listened to the various hypotheses of the researchers, I reminded myself to "not totally believe what people tell you." In this case, it meant that I should question the accuracy of the information that was being taken as factual. I questioned the accuracy of the research process temperature measurements and proposed a way to test their validity since they could not be directly verified. My test was conducted and it confirmed that the temperature measurements were in error. It was amazing in this case that almost two years of research had been conducted, at great financial expense to the corporation, and the results were useless. All because the researchers were willing to propose elaborate hypotheses for why their results did not match the commercial reality rather than question basic information upon which their conclusions were based. This is why an innovator has to develop his/her own information rather than "believe what people tell him/her."

Chapter 15

Complex Innovations Accomplished in Steps

Just as Rome was not built in a day,
complex innovations are not completed
all at once; but rather result from
successful steps – one upon another.

Complex innovations require that success be achieved in steps, versus all at once.

♦ Successful innovation resulting from "the big idea" can be complex and thus require thinking creatively in terms of steps – steps defined in terms of milestones, and timelines for accomplishment of the milestones.

♦ Since complex innovations usually involve multiple technologies, the innovator must focus on achieving several milestones while combining these into a coherent plan for total success of the project.

♦ Working in terms of steps will take time requiring patience on the part of both the innovator and the sponsoring organization.

♦ Developing skills using the many planning and organizing tools available will prove essential for success.

♦ Achieving success from complex innovations involving multiple technologies requires the innovator to be skilled at working on, or leading, a team.

Complex Innovations Accomplished in Steps

Development projects at major corporations are set up with timelines for accomplishment of milestones, with each milestone being a step along the way to project success. Complex projects require a number of steps. Therefore, we need to think creatively in terms of steps. It is like winning a baseball game with singles and doubles versus home runs. It is like winning a football game with short yardage runs versus long passing bombs. Complex innovations require the team approach, especially now in the 21st century where the projects combine interdisciplinary talent and skill for success.

The speed of innovation certainly accelerated throughout the 20th century, to the point where now in the 21st century it is difficult for organizations to be patient for complex innovations to be completed. It is even difficult for individual innovators to be patient. We want it all done – and done right now! But things are just not that simple. And when faced with complex innovations and needing new ideas and creativity to keep things going – sometimes we have to just let it happen (see Chapter 5). But for complex innovations, the "just letting it happen" approach takes on another dimension; thus, we must think in terms of steps – each step of the innovation building upon the other ones. Our creative thinking must be compartmentalized so that we focus on developing creative ideas for each step that we have laid out in an overall plan.

Technology development in the 21st century will indeed be complex and involve what is referred to as the intersection of specific technologies. Examples of intersections could include applying fluid mechanics engineering to biological processes or applying high voltage physics to making new nano-scale materials. The development of creative concepts at the intersection of technologies requires general knowledge of the multiple technologies involved. It will take time for innovators to acquire the additional baseline knowledge needed for new concept development, and therefore thinking in terms of steps will be a useful technique for focusing on getting only the knowledge that is needed. Both the innovator and the sponsoring organization must demonstrate patience for this technique to be successful.

Personal Experience

The projects I worked on early in my career were such that I could attain successful innovation by working as an individual. Later in my career, the innovations became more complex and I had to transition from the individual approach to the team approach. I was a team member on some projects and a team leader on other projects. As I learned to function as a team member and team leader, I became familiar with the concurrent engineering (CE) method and found it to be extremely effective. Part of the CE process is identifying the specific requirements of the customer, i.e., the user of the innovation being developed. The CE process also establishes a metric of success for each specific or functional requirement. The CE process can be applied to establish design specifications for process innovation. As the name implies, work is carried on concurrently on the various disciplines involved and on the various steps of the innovation according to an overall development plan. Thus CE is ideal for complex innovations accomplished in steps at the intersections of technologies.

I used the CE process on two exceedingly difficult innovations – both of which required innovations combining multidisciplinary technologies. Both projects were staffed by about 20 engineers and scientists. I found that CE enabled creativeness and fostered excellent teamwork, while keeping the development timeline on schedule.

Chapter 16

Developing Multiple Paths to Success

Only the foolhardy novice
relies on one path for success.

Always develop multiple paths to success with as many back-ups as possible.

♦ Turning a creative idea into a successful innovation is a journey that usually takes many paths.

♦ Successful innovators develop multiple back-up paths to go along with their original primary path.

♦ The ability to simultaneously work along parallel paths and exchange ideas and results among the paths will enhance the chance of success.

♦ Successful innovation is a non-linear process using creative ideas developed from pursuing multiple paths.

Developing Multiple Paths to Success

Turning creative ideas and concepts into successful innovations requires that many paths be developed and explored. To rely on one path to success is foolhardy and has no doubt led to the failure of many, many innovations. It is easy to get locked into pursuing only one path for several reasons: 1) training in engineering and science generally teaches that there is one answer to classroom problems and that translates into pursuing that "one answer" via a single path, 2) a tremendous amount of work and dedication are required to work on multiple paths or work streams concurrently, and 3) working on multiple paths can be viewed as non-focused effort by the innovator's manager, hence forcing the one path approach. Developing and pursuing multiple paths does not mean that any less effort is directed toward the primary path, it just means that more effort has to be expended.

Businesses have contingency planning as part of their business plan. Why then should innovators not have back-up plans, or alternate paths, as part of their development plan? To be successful at innovation, alternate paths have to be developed. They must be worked on simultaneously to enhance the chance of success. Creative ideas can be exchanged across these multiple paths, leading to a superior development plan for the primary path. Sometimes an alternate path will become the primary path and be better than the original primary path. In fact, if you accept that anything can be done and that success has to be attained, then you might argue that a back-up plan has to be as good, or better, than the primary plan. While this may sound a little off-the-wall, consider a sky diver with a primary parachute and a back-up parachute. If the primary parachute does not deploy, then does not the back-up parachute become the more important one? Approaching successful innovation from this perspective will drive the innovator to development of superior back-up plans leading to a greater chance of success.

Personal Experience

I have been involved in many development projects where success could be accomplished in several technical ways. Of course when I started working on these projects I did not know the various ways that success could be attained. It was due to the effort of developing the primary path and the back-up paths, and working on these simultaneously, that I discovered the various ways. Sometimes it was years later, following successful implementation of one path, that I discovered that another path existed all along. The possibility of the existence of another path to success is difficult to explain to most people. This is because we all seem to want to believe there is just one way to do or accomplish something, especially once that something has been achieved and is working well. Nevertheless my experiences have reinforced my view that the successful innovator should always be developing multiple paths to success no matter how well the work is going on the primary path.

We all are aware of products developed by different companies that address the same consumer need. Each company will use a different technology or process to make their product. Thus it is evident that success can be achieved in multiple ways. Therefore, I am suggesting that the innovator search and find alternate paths to solving his/her problem statement (project) because a simpler one probably exists and will lead to faster successful innovation.

Today, I always look to develop multiple paths to success for every project I undertake and advise my clients to do the same. I would not think of working on a project unless I had a back-up plan. This approach extends beyond scientific projects and applies to all facets of life's experiences.

Chapter 17

Value of Setting Intermediate Milestones

The practicality of turning creativity into successful innovation means that deadlines are a necessary part of the process.

Measure your success by setting a few intermediate milestones to coincide with a step-by-step approach.

♦ Home runs are hard to hit, singles and doubles are easier; and likewise, accomplishment of an overall successful innovation is sometimes best done by achievement of intermediate steps along the way.

♦ Setting a deadline for accomplishment of each step helps the innovator be successful by imparting a sense of urgency to his/her work that helps him/her focus his/her efforts.

♦ Turning creativity into successful innovation is not a linear process, therefore the innovator must learn to work on multiple steps and deadlines simultaneously.

♦ The feeling that progress is being made is a large part of successful innovation, thus accomplishing intermediate milestones maintains project momentum.

♦ Changing intermediate milestones and deadlines are part of the process of successful innovation – changing the ultimate milestone of project success is not part of the process.

Value of Setting Intermediate Milestones

The milestones for a project are divided into two kinds: 1) the ultimate milestone of the project and business success, and 2) the intermediate milestones, the accomplishment of which are foreseen as necessary to accomplishing the ultimate milestone. Development projects at major corporations in the 21st century are structured in terms of accomplishing both ultimate and intermediate milestones corresponding to a timeline. The more complex the project, the greater the number of intermediate milestones and deadlines for the innovator to accomplish. This is a good way to do things. It enables the innovator to focus his/her efforts and maintain project momentum corresponding to the accomplishment of the milestones. Accomplishing milestones also enables project funding to continue when the innovator is working for a large corporation or organization.

Ultimately, there is only one milestone – accomplishing business success resulting from a successful innovation. The setting of intermediate milestones and deadlines is of course only a formalized process to assist the innovator in accomplishing the ultimate business success. However, the total process is not a linear one; but rather a convoluted journey that is nonlinear. There are many lateral tasks that arise and many multiple paths that must be explored. This means that formal milestones must be changed, and accordingly the old deadlines missed. The structure of major corporations makes this a difficult task because it can appear that the project is in trouble and may not be successful. Thus, the innovator experiences great personal stress and the creative ideas required to change course and set new milestones and deadlines are hard to come by. This book is dedicated to the quest for better ideas when needed and advice for dealing with the personal stress associated with maintaining "a wanting to do it" attitude for accomplishing a successful innovation.

Personal Experience

As I have stated herein before, I have always been comfortable with being at risk; thus changing the milestones has always been relatively easy for me to do. But I have never changed an ultimate milestone because I believe that anything can be accomplished. In my experience, this is the most important factor when setting milestones: maintain your focus on accomplishing the ultimate milestone of project success. Accordingly, I have experienced all anxieties associated with the innovation process at a major corporation or organization and know first hand just how difficult the journey is. Setting a few intermediate milestones and deadlines has helped me to be successful because it focuses the creative process and builds project momentum when some milestones are achieved.

An experience with the value of setting and accomplishing intermediate milestones happened to me when working on a very complex project requiring several innovations. I set a few intermediate milestones, and deadlines for accomplishing the milestones; both for myself and the team I was leading. As the milestones were accomplished, I could see the dramatic positive effect on our team's behavior and morale. These successes along the way reinforced our dedication to achieving success of the ultimate project and business milestone. I am convinced that we were able to maintain this positive approach and vision throughout the course of the project by the establishment of intermediate milestones.

An experience with the value of setting an ultimate milestone, and never deviating from the focus that it absolutely had to be accomplished, happened to me when scaling up commercial processes to significantly increase production rates. As discussed in Chapter 2, it was a time of great personal stress and career risk for me; however, knowing that the requirement of ultimate project success would never be changed was a source of strength for me as I sought out new ideas on how to solve the problem I encountered. This is when I learned that total support of one's organization is so helpful to the innovator during the struggle to accomplish an ultimate milestone of significant business success, and that changing the ultimate milestone is not a part of the successful innovation process.

Chapter 18

Diversity of Side Projects

An innovator's greatest successes
frequently result from his/her side projects.

Practice diversity in thinking by always having side projects.

♦ Creativity can be enhanced and restored by breaking away from primary projects and developing side projects.

♦ The "flow" associated with starting up a side project feeds back into renewed energy and creativity that can be applied into the primary project.

♦ Side projects frequently turn into primary projects and may actually bring the innovator the greatest successes.

♦ Having a potential side project innovation "on the shelf" enables the successful innovator to "out run their Innovation Development Curve" which means that the innovator achieves success faster than called for by his/her plan.

Value of Side Projects

Taking a break or a respite from an intense effort aimed at making a project successful restores one's energy and focus. A good way to take a break is to have a couple of side projects going simultaneously with your primary project. The side project has the benefit of not having a schedule attached to it. You can work on it with a very open mind. It is always there in the background. You can envision success without actually having any effort going on – it's a mental thing to some extent, which of course is the value of it in the first place. Thus, you diversify your thinking. But as you put some effort into the side project, you will find that good things can happen on the primary project. The techniques put forth in this book will help you get into a state of natural "flow" without having to focus on the application of the techniques. This state of "flow" is extremely important – it can lead to the serendipity factor entering into your work. In other words, good ideas can come from anywhere when you are just letting great ideas happen. This is when you are striving for creative ideas at a higher level and you could truly get "out-of-the-box." You may find that new ideas occur to you that can be fed back into your primary project.

As the 21st century starts to unfold, development projects are getting more complex due to the intersection of many technologies – various types of engineering, biology, chemistry, medicine, computational capacity, and so on. This means that the chances are high for the innovator to be assigned projects adjacent to his/her primary training discipline. Thus, he/she may not be as successful working in these arenas as he/she would be working in his/her primary field of training and career choice. Developing side projects requiring more direct use of his/her talent and training should be a stimulus to his/her energy and creativity.

Another interesting thing is that side projects often turn into primary projects. Senior professionals have a way of making this happen and it is viewed as a necessary part of a successful technology organization. In this manner, senior professionals "define their own jobs" and can "outrun their own Innovation Development Curve" by having a side project turn into a major project.

Personal Experience

During my tenure with the DuPont Company, many of my side projects turned into my primary projects and ended up bringing me the most success. Looking back, it is truly amazing that this happened. My first experience with this came about early in my DuPont career when I started running aerodynamic experiments outside the scope of my primary assignment which was unrelated to aerodynamics. While I did not recognize it at that time, I was using my core technical training and skills to develop a side project. I continued to work full-time on my primary assignment and kept working extra time on the side project. As things progressed, I ended up working in the aerodynamics arena on my primary projects and it led to my greatest successes at DuPont.

As my career has progressed, I have always managed to have as many side projects going as possible. As stated above, I find that digressing into another area away from my main focus area renews my creative thinking. It also provides me with a stimulus leading to greater energy to focus and work on my primary activities. I never had anyone criticize me for working this way and I thought that it was part of what I should be doing as a professional engineer and employee. The key point to realize is that when you are working for a large corporation or organization, the side projects obviously have to be in the best interest of the corporation or organization. Any side project meeting this criterion should be worthy of the innovator's effort.

Chapter 19

Striving for Creative Ideas at a Higher Level

When success is in sight,
creativity can be taken to its highest level
by applying the same perseverance and
determination required to overcome
the difficult periods.

Always be striving for creative ideas at a higher level – especially when things are going well.

♦ The best time for an innovator is when things are progressing well; however, it is also the ideal time to extend the creative idea to a higher level.

♦ Extend ideas to a higher creative level by seeking simpler or more robust approaches.

♦ Seek collaboration with other experts and practice their techniques for extending the application of the idea at hand to get truly "out-of-the-box."

♦ Look at problems in their component parts and look at all aspects of test results as sources of positive inputs for developing creative ideas.

♦ Have a brainstorming session based on positive results as opposed to overcoming problems based on negative results.

Striving for Creative Ideas at a Higher Level

When things are going well in your innovation work, these are the best of times; and this is when you need to take your work to the next level. The same thing exists in playing sports – you achieve a certain level of expertise at a sport and then to become truly great, the athlete must "go to the next level" so-to-speak. Another way to think of this is to deliver more from your creativity than what is expected. Ask yourself, "How can I attain a more successful innovation with more impact than what is being sought?" Or ask yourself, "How can the creative idea be extended to other adjacent fields of endeavor?"

You may want to start thinking about a simpler approach or perhaps a more robust approach. Think about additional applications of your work. Do some collaborative discussions with other experts in the field – pick their brains, especially when you know that you have something that is going to work and be successful. Add to your work. Make it better. Extend it. Try to practice the techniques of other innovators, superimposed upon your already successful "base approach" that got you this far. Try to truly "get-out-of-box." Listen to other people – ask them for input. Ask the "man-on-the-street" question – what would someone that is not familiar with your innovation do if you explained to them that you wanted to extend the work? This is sort of the opposite of the situation in Chapter 13 where we asked the "man-on-the-street" to help us with a difficult situation – now we are asking for assistance to improve a positive situation.

A new concept is to have a brainstorming session when things are going very well. An outline for an effective brainstorming session in order to get back on the innovation development curve is presented in Chapter 9. I have modified that outline (as presented below) for the "positive" brainstorming session. During this "positive" brainstorming session, emphasize visualization of project success – what does it look like? Have each participant describe in 3D and in color what they visualize. Also have each participant do some projections of the innovation into adjacent areas where it may be applicable. It could be a back-up plan for the adjacent area.

Outline for a "Positive" Brainstorming Meeting
(How to Take a Successful Innovation to a Higher Level)

1) *Develop the problem statement*
    a) Review project functional requirements, i.e., QFD
    b) Rack-up relevant data and trends
    c) Each participant presents an assessment of their problem statement
    d) Define a consensus problem statement

2) *Define the problem constraints*
    a) Led by group leader and experts in the area

3) *Relax the problem constraints*
    a) Participants develop ideas
    b) Participants present their ideas to the group

4) *Each participant develops an explanation of the problem for the "man-on-the-street"*
   a) Each participant presents their explanation to the group

5) *Each participant develops an idea for the simplest thing that can be done*
   a) Each participant presents their idea to the group

6) *Each participant develops an "out-of-the-box" idea*
   a) Each participant presents their idea to the group

7) *Each participant develops a back-up plan*
   a) Each participant presents their back-up plan to the group

8) *Determine if the project can be approached in terms of steps*
   a) Group discussion
   b) Determine the steps to be taken if the project can be approached in steps

9) *Visualize project success – define what it looks like*
   a) Determine if anything can be compromised and look for application of the 80-20 rule

10) *Document the output from the meeting and develop the path forward for the innovator*

Personal Experience

A great portion of this book is dedicated to dealing with the difficult times encountered by converting creativity into successful innovation; however, I have found that when things were going well in my work, that was my best time as a creative person. It also gives you time and a chance to build upon the work of colleagues and maybe extend their work by helping them. This happened to me once when I was able to apply an aerodynamic principle to an innovation being developed by a colleague. The resulting idea took his innovation to a higher level and enabled him to make proof of concept samples and sustain progress.

Chapter 20

Thinking the Right Kinds of Thoughts

To a great extent, an innovator achieves
success by thinking positively, exhibiting
a high degree of flexibility, and taking
immediate bold action when needed.

Success results from thinking the right kinds of thoughts, doing the right things, and making the right decisions.

♦ Being positive, focusing on success as opposed to avoiding failure, being flexible and not linear, and believing all things are possible – these are examples of the right kinds of thoughts.

♦ Developing aggressive schedules, behaving as a team player versus individualistically, openly sharing results as they are obtained, and taking responsibility – these are examples of doing the right things.

♦ Seeking feedback that assists iteration and improvement, not hesitating to make changes as needed, practicing the 80-20 rule, and working in a transparent manner with team members – these are examples of skills that help with making the right decisions.

♦ An innovator who practices these behaviors has the greatest chance for success.

Thinking the Right Kinds of Thoughts and Doing the Right Things

The approach of working in a conservative, avoiding failure posture will almost certainly be self-fulfilling. Following the scientific method, using core training in the sciences and engineering, and practicing good business principles, should be viewed as only part of the innovator's tool kit – alone they will not assure success. Turning creativity into the reality of successful innovation requires bold action, the continual state of being at risk, and the underlying belief that all things are possible. It is a given and absolutely essential that successful innovators be positive thinkers with a high degree of flexibility in their decision making.

Developing aggressive schedules and stretch goals are good things to do for both the individual innovator and a team. In either case, the development process will be aided along by the immediate sharing of results so that iteration can occur and be fed back into the schedule and status of the project. Thus, working in a transparent manner is extremely important. Taking personal responsibility for one's share of the work load has to be part of the behavior of the successful innovator.

Seeking feedback, as results are openly discussed, will assist the iterative process that has to occur during the development process. The successful innovator will be flexible and not hesitate to make changes that are needed to increase the chance of project success. Always strive to follow the 80-20 rule, which states that often

80% of the total result can be attained from 20% of the right focused effort. Attaining technical perfection is impossible and should not be strived for; instead, work toward the 80-20 effect.

Personal Experience

I have found that few people practice the combination of behaviors required to think the right kinds of thoughts and make the right decisions required to be a successful innovator. The world values the truly great innovators because there are not many of them. It is, therefore, left for the rest of us to strive to practice as many of the right behaviors as we can. It takes practice, and in my case, I have been striving and learning for a lifetime. I have had the good fortune to work for a company that valued my work and gave me an opportunity to practice many of the behaviors required to turn my creative ideas into successful realities.

While I have talked of many things so far in this book, I have not stressed the importance of transparency as applied to the open sharing of results as they are attained in the course of technical work and experimental investigations. This behavioral trait does require a great deal of personal confidence and one has to be in a supportive environment where continual criticism does not occur. The immediate sharing of results, and the iteration process that followed, played a large part in the success of many of my projects. I did not approach this sharing of results from any "internal political perspective," but rather from the viewpoint that interesting and often unexpected results were worth immediate discussion among my peers and colleagues.

At each point in my career at DuPont, I had at least one close colleague with whom I could share results of tests and develop new ideas. Looking back, these interactions were important in that they helped me learn how to think the right kinds of thoughts and to make good decisions. These relationships were based on trust and mutual respect. As a result, I became a person that shared data openly, when I took it, and was totally transparent. I am convinced that these behaviors helped me achieve my success at DuPont. When I encounter an innovator at a large organization that works in an insular manner, I know that he/she is limiting their chances for success. I think that this type of behavior would similarly limit innovators in all areas of endeavor; business, arts, education, …

Chapter 21

Making the Right Decisions

Most of life's successes result from making
the right decisions along the way.

Thinking the right kinds of thoughts keeps you in the game, doing the right things and making the right decisions win the game.

♦ Successful innovators bundle a package of behaviors and choices that lead to making good decisions.

♦ To be successful, you must win the game (so-to-speak) by putting innovations into commercial practice. To do this, many personal traits and skills are required of the innovator beyond those dealing strictly with innovation and creativity.

♦ The highest personal trait is a high degree of ethics which the innovator never compromises, even if it means enduring setbacks along the way to winning the game.

♦ While this book has stated that continually being at risk is a necessary part of the innovation process – as success is within sight, the successful innovator must make the right decision by reducing the state of risk and taking only the conservative, prudent risks required to win the game.

Making the Right Decisions

Commercial and business successes are the scorecards for the innovator. Turning creative ideas into successful innovations means that useful things result that are valued by the world's population. Achieving a successful innovation is, therefore an extremely difficult task, accomplished by relatively few in history. Innovators are rare, but they do have in common the ability to make the right decisions that lead to the success of their particular innovations. In this book I have put forth what I think are the behaviors, skills, and choices that one has to practice to be a successful innovator and "win your particular game."

The package of behaviors for making the right decisions includes practicing the highest level of professional and ethical standards. This is a core personal attribute in that an innovator never takes credit for another person's work. Respect from your colleagues and your business and professional communities comes from practicing uncompromised ethics. Good ethics make for good decisions.

While being at risk is necessary in the pursuit of successful innovation, it's another matter when the right decision has to be made to win the game by achieving commercial success. With success in the balance, the innovator must make the right decisions and take the minimum risks necessary for project completion. Business success trumps the attempt at achieving technical perfection.

Personal Experience

I have been fortunate to have made some very good decisions in my life and career, as well as to have had serendipity play a part now and then. My life started with two instances of serendipity:

1) I was born to parents that encouraged me to get an education, and

2) They lived within commuting distance of Virginia Tech.

When I was in my senior year of college, I was fortunate to get a job with the Boeing Company working on the Apollo Program. Being a rocket man was my childhood dream, and I had finally realized the dream. That experience changed my life by making me realize that dreams can come true, and that anything that can be imagined can be accomplished! It formed my lifelong positive attitude and willingness to take appropriate career risks to accomplish successful innovation.

Following Apollo, I made an extremely difficult decision to exit the space program and leave Huntsville, Alabama to pursue my Ph.D. degree. It was during that time that I gained confidence that I could do research work. Then I got a job at DuPont, which came about in a completely serendipitous way. A fellow graduate student had a job offer from DuPont in the area of fluids, whereas his major was stress analysis, and I thought "if they are offering him a job in an adjacent field, then I surely have a chance since I was majoring in fluids." I never thought that an aerodynamics engineer would work for a "chemical" company. Of course, I would come to learn that working at DuPont was another dream job for me because, for most of my 34 years there, I was DuPont's only "rocket scientist!" And as acknowledged previously, it was at DuPont that I learned and formulated the techniques presented in this book. For most of my years at DuPont, I experienced a supportive environment which is absolutely essential for creativity and successful innovation. Without that supportive environment, this book would have never been written.

Therefore, it's incredible how apparently insignificant decisions and choices at the time can have such far ranging impacts on one's life and career. For me, each change in direction has first created a sense of great hope for the future. Then, there has followed a period of adjustment in which I had to work through many difficulties realizing that I was in a state of great personal risk. Each time I wondered if I had made the right decision. During these periods of difficulty, I found that perseverance and dedication to do the right things led to my emergence with better skills to attempt innovation as a career option. This is why I opened this book with the statement:

You have to put at risk both your creative ideas and your career
in order to have one of life's most exhilarating experiences
– *successful innovation, accomplished after persevering and
overcoming all the obstacles and frustration along the way.*

May you turn all your creative ideas into successful innovations!

Coming Next

Dr. Marshall will interview a cross-section of the world's greatest innovators and most creative people in order to learn their techniques for success. The results will comprise the basis for his next book in this series on creativity and innovation.

About the Author

Dr. Marshall graduated from Virginia Tech in 1966 with a degree in Aerospace Engineering and began his professional career with the Boeing Company working on the Apollo Moon Landing Project. Following receipt of his Master's Degree in 1970 from the University of Alabama in Huntsville, he returned to Virginia Tech and received his Ph.D. Degree in Engineering Science and Mechanics in 1974. Dr. Marshall then started his 34 year career with the DuPont Company, retiring in 2008 as a DuPont Fellow – DuPont's highest research position. Throughout his career, Dr. Marshall has been known for his positive thinking and high level of personal creativity. These traits translated into a R&D success rate of greater than 70% during his DuPont career – an almost unheard of success rate when the widely regarded norm is 10%! Dr. Marshall holds 12 U.S. Patents.

Today Dr. Marshall is President of Marshall Consulting LLC, a company devoted to the practice of the techniques presented in this book. Dr. Marshall also holds the position of Senior R&D Fellow in Residence at Huvard Research and Consulting, Inc.

10334211R00093

Made in the USA
Charleston, SC
27 November 2011